Get Active.
Active Teaching Ideas
For Lifetime Learning
Kurt·Bickel

Edited by Arnold E. Schmidt

Copyright © 1997 Concordia Publishing House
3558 South Jefferson Avenue, St. Louis, MO 63118-3968
Manufactured in the United States of America

This publication is also available in braille and in large print for the visually impaired. Write to Library for the Blind, 1333 South Kirkwood Road, St. Louis, MO 63122-7295; or call 1-800-433-3954.

Contents

Introduction   4

1   The Art of Teaching the Faith   11

2   Balanced Teaching   17

3   The Learner   25

4   Teacher Readiness   39

5   Active Learning   45

6   Active Learning Designs: Early Childhood   57

7   Active Learning Designs: Primary   67

8   Active Learning Designs: Intermediate   77

9   Active Learning Designs: Middle
    School to Adult   87

10 Design Your Own Active Learning   95

    Conditions for Credit   107

    Application for Credit   108

Introduction

We would like to see Jesus. (John 12:21)

In the gospel of John we read how some Greeks had come to Philip, the disciple, with a request. "Sir," they said, "we would like to see Jesus." Philip went to tell Andrew; Andrew and Philip in turn told Jesus. Jesus referred to a kernel of wheat in His answer to this request. He was speaking about His death and glorification. Then the Greeks and the crowd heard a thunderous voice from heaven (John 12:20–30).

Helping people to "see" Jesus is a privilege like few others. Christian teachers are acting in faith by teaching the Word of God to young people. They are partners with parents who have promised to bring up their children in the nurture and admonition of the Lord. By their efforts and through the power of the Holy Spirit faith is nurtured. Teachers may not have thunderous voices. Yet as God's Spirit works through the powerful Word they share, they have a positive life-changing effect upon the world. Christian teachers are the living witnesses of Jesus, the One who, like the kernel of wheat, died to produce new life in all people.

This book is written with a great appreciation and respect for everyone who teaches the Word of God and helps others "see" Jesus. Its goal is to help teachers use a variety of methods to teach the faith.

PROFOUND MESSAGE REQUIRES DIVERSE METHODS

The Gospel message from God is a great paradox of simplicity and complexity. The message can be as simple as, "God is Love" (1 John 4:8). St. John also states, "Jesus did many other things as well. If every one of them were written down, I suppose that even the whole world would not have room for the books that would be written" (John 21:25).

This book about active learning celebrates Christian education with its profound simplicity and complexity. It underscores the power of the Spirit to work faith when methods as diverse as creation itself are used to present the Gospel of Christ. Think of the Bible as the textbook, Jesus as the subject, and faith as the object. The result? By God's grace and with His power working through the Word, the lives of learners will become lives of worship, culminating an eternity of bliss with the Savior.

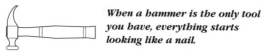 *When a hammer is the only tool you have, everything starts looking like a nail.*

Special skills and tools enhance the teaching of the faith. The best teaching is a balance of many methods and styles..

ACTIVE LEARNING

Try this:

    Handle an apple or another piece of fruit.

    List everything you can about the apple (color, texture, smell, what it's made of, etc.)

    Cross out the items from the list that you could not discover if you could only see a picture of an apple.

    Cross out items if you could only hear the word *apple.*

    What does this say about the way children learn?

Or, try this:

    Draw seven index cards on a sheet of paper in any configuration. (See sample.)

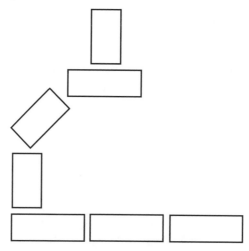

Using only words, ask a friend to reproduce your drawing. Do not give hints with your hands or in any other way, and do not allow your friend to see your drawing.

We learn more about an object when we have the benefit of using the real thing instead of a picture and when we can use the senses of smell, touch, sight, and hearing instead of just one or two senses. Likewise, we can accomplish a simple task more easily and with more accuracy when we can use more than one of our senses. Active learning involves the use of our senses.

At times active learning may look chaotic: noisy students, out of their chairs. Children, in groups on the floor, talk and laugh. At times the teacher appears to be only passively involved. Instead of leading and telling, she may be simply listening and observing. Children are measuring and experimenting. They are competing in teams and cheering for their side.

Look closely; look carefully; this is learning the way kids learn. Listen closely; this is how children practice faith talk. Look, listen, and learn. The teacher is using carefully planned activities. The spirit of enthusiasm is present in the active learning classroom. A spirit of imagination is being cultivated. The Spirit of God is moving, shaping faith, and transforming lives.

The God of creation has designed the world with diversity and variety. People, like their fingerprints, are all different. A wide variety of teaching tools can help teachers reach the diverse learners in their classroom as they teach the faith in dynamic ways. In learning situations variety is more than the "spice of life"; it's more like the meat and potatoes of successful teaching. Active learning is a nonlinear education process. Most books are designed to be linear. This book, however, will encourage the reader to explore beyond these pages with models, exercises, and experiences that will make it an active learning process.

Chapter 1 will include a discussion about the nature of teaching the faith.

Chapter 2 provides information about how to achieve a balance in teaching.

Chapter 3 will take an extensive look at the learner by exploring the age-level characteristics and different learning styles. There is good reason to teach children with active learning techniques.

Chapter 4 will include opportunities for the reader to reflect upon their readiness for teaching in an active learning style.

In Chapter 5 active learning is defined in detail.

Chapters 6–9 provide suggestions to help you use active learning in your classroom.

Designs for Early Childhood (6)
Designs for Primary (7)
Designs for Intermediate (8)
Designs for Middle School to Adult (9)

Chapter 10 shows how to design your own active learning experiences and provides additional ideas.

ASK ME TO DANCE

Praise the LORD! Praise God in His sanctuary; praise Him in His mighty heavens. Praise Him for His acts of power; praise Him for His surpassing greatness. Praise Him with the sounding of the trumpet, praise Him with the harp and lyre, praise Him with tambourine and dancing, praise Him with strings and flute, praise Him with the clash of cymbals, praise Him with resounding cymbals. Let everything that has breath praise the LORD. Praise the LORD. (Psalm 150)

Amazing grace! How sweet the sound That saved a wretch like me!

Can you read these words without hearing the music?

When you hear the music to your favorite waltz or a two-step, isn't it hard not to move? Well, it is for me!

By now, you must have guessed, I am a *right-brained, feeling/doer, intuitive learner.* (See Chapter 3.)

I also have a pronounced case of dyslexia (thank God for spell check). I experienced school as a less than happy place. School lifted up the things that were wrong with me. It was worse in Sunday school.

I remember thinking. I want to be a teacher who helps kids like me.

> In school they asked me to read and to stand when I
>   couldn't.
> In school they asked me to spell and said you must
>   not have studied.
> In school they asked me to add, subtract, and divide,
>   but sometimes the 6's were 9's.
> In Sunday school they asked me to recite passages,
>   and I seldom could do it.
> In Sunday school they asked me to fill out worksheets,
>   and I never finished.
> In Sunday school they always went around the circle
>   to read the Bible. I looked ahead to find my pas-
>   sage.
> But no one asked me to dance!

Cognitive study is like knowing the words.
Affective imagination is like hearing the music.
Psychomotor artwork is like dancing with joy.
Someone ask me to dance.

Thanks to Arnold Schmidt, Jim Gimbel, and the people at Concordia Publishing House for letting me celebrate God's grace through active learning. Yes, I would love to dance!

Kurt Bickel

The Art of Teaching
the Faith

For it is by grace you have been saved, through faith—and this not from yourselves, it is the gift of God—not by works, so that no one can boast. For we are God's workmanship, created in Christ Jesus to do good works, which God prepared in advance for us to do. (Ephesians 2:8–10)

Teaching the faith is not an applied science. It is an art form born of faith in Jesus. The Christian faith is more than knowing about God. Faith is a relationship established by God as He draws us to Himself and as He brings us to trust and live for Him. The Holy

Spirit causes faith to grow as individuals hear and receive the Gospel message (Romans 10:17).

We do not share the love of Jesus in a vacuum. We meet people where they are—just as Jesus did. He often used active learning methods to teach about spiritual matters. For example, when He taught about humility in Mark 9:32–37, He took a little child and had him stand among them. When Jesus blessed little children, He put His hands on them (Mark 10:16). Jesus used the object lesson of His healing of a blind man to teach about spiritual blindness (John 9:35–41). When Thomas doubted that Jesus had risen from the dead, Jesus told him, "Put your finger here; see My hands. Reach out your hand and put it into My side" (John 20:27).

KNOWLEDGE, UNDERSTANDING, AND WISDOM

While faith is first and foremost a relationship with God, faith does involve knowledge, understanding, and wisdom. Examine these words from St. Paul to the Colossians:

We always thank God, the Father of our Lord Jesus Christ, when we pray for you, because we have heard of your faith in Christ Jesus and of the love you have for all the saints—the faith and love that spring from the hope that is stored up for you in heaven and that you have already heard about in the word of truth, the gospel that has come to you. All over the world the gospel is bearing fruit and growing, just as it has been doing among you since the day you heard it and understood God's grace in all its truth. You learned it from Epaphras, our dear fellow servant, who is a faithful minister of Christ on our behalf, and who also told us of your love in the Spirit. For this reason, since the day we heard about you, we have not stopped praying for you and asking God to fill you with the knowledge of His will through all spiritual wisdom and understanding. And we pray this in order that you may live a life worthy of the Lord and may please Him in every way: bearing fruit in every good work, growing in the knowledge of God. (Colossians 1:3–10)

This passage speaks of many different levels of "understanding" God. St. Paul speaks of the Colossians' faith in Christ, their love for all the saints, and of the hope they have in heaven. How did this great faith happen? The word of truth, the Gospel, came to them and from the day they heard it they understood God's grace. They *learned* it from Epaphras. Still, Paul's prayer for them is that they will be filled with the *knowledge* of God's will through all *spiritual wisdom* and *understanding.* He prays for this because he wants them to lead lives worthy of the Lord and so that they will bear fruit.

The answer to the question "Does an understanding of God lead to faith in God?" is no. Greater knowledge and understanding of God is not what works faith; faith takes root and grows only as the Holy Spirit works faith through the Word of God. The adage "Faith is not taught; it is caught" contains more than a kernel of truth. Like a bush catching on fire, faith is more than intellectual assent. It is a total experience of heart, soul, and mind.

Faith in God leads to greater understanding of God.

As Christian teachers we tell the word of truth just as Epaphras did so that the Gospel can come into the hearts of our students. As Christian teachers we also have a calling to help our students grow in the knowledge, understanding, and wisdom of God's will.

Exercise

Think of something you have learned recently, such as programming a VCR; using a new computer program; or preparing a meal, using a new and difficult recipe. Now that you have something in mind, rate yourself on the following scale.

1	2	3	4	5	6	7	8	9	10
I know it			I understand it			I am wise concerning it.			

This exercise demonstrates that *understanding* is more valuable than *knowledge,* and that *wisdom* is even more valuable.

Listen to the writer of the Proverbs, "For the LORD gives wisdom; From His mouth come knowledge and understanding. He stores up sound wisdom for the upright; He is a shield to those who walk uprightly" (Proverbs 2:6–7 NKJV).

The Old Testament is clear about teaching and learning. We learn about God's wondrous works so that we might know them. As God gives us understanding and wisdom, He also empowers us to live according to His will. Wisdom shows itself in the way we live.

Note the references to knowledge, understanding, and wisdom in Psalm 119.

The book of James says it this way, "Who is wise and understanding among you? Let him show it by his good life, by deeds done in the humility that comes from wisdom" (James 3:13).

Wisdom in God Involves Action

If the one who is wise in the faith is one who lives it out, Christian educators do well to focus their teaching on action. Active learning emphasizes being and doing, not just thinking and feeling. Think about how you teach or would like to teach. Toward which side do you lean?

Emotional	Logical
Inductive	Deductive
Feeling	Thinking
Application	Meditation
Experiential	Descriptions
Affective	Cognitive
Student Active	**Student Passive**
Teacher Passive	**Teacher Active**

TEACHING THE FAITH REQUIRES BALANCE OF ALL SIDES

Have you been using active learning methods when you teach? If not, are you ready to provide balance for your lessons by including some active methods? You must actually do active learning in order to grow in your understanding of it and of the benefits it can provide. We will discuss this in greater detail in chapter 4.

God's wisdom comes to us and goes out from us in active love. Christ's life, death, and resurrection are not passive ideas but real action by a real person: Jesus. Teaching actively celebrates the wisdom of God. Excellent Christian teaching always focuses on the cross and the great act of sacrificial love Jesus did there for us.

Where is the wise man? Where is the scholar? Where is the philosopher of this age? Has not God made foolish the wisdom of the world? For since in the wisdom of God the world through its wisdom did not know him, God was pleased through the foolishness of what was preached to save those who believe. Jews demand miraculous signs and Greeks look for wisdom, but we preach Christ crucified: a stumbling block to Jews and foolishness to Gentiles, but to those whom God has called, both Jews and Greeks, Christ the power of God and the wisdom of God. For the foolishness of God is wiser than man's wisdom, and the weakness of God is stronger than man's strength. (1 Corinthians 1:20–25)

Balanced Teaching

Thus also faith by itself, if it does not have works, is dead.
(James 2:17 NKJV)

COMPREHENSION AND APPREHENSION

Comprehension. Have you ever experienced a time when you had to separate yourself from a problem before you could solve it? Perhaps you said, "I need to think about it." When that occurs, you utilize an *indirect understanding* called comprehension.

Apprehension. Recall a time when you have experienced a new focus by "putting yourself in someone else's shoes." Or, think of a time when you were unable to understand something until you actually did it. In this situation you are using a direct understanding called apprehension.

These two types of thinking processes go together. The interaction of the two processes in our conscience leads to what we would recognize as learning. Comprehension and apprehension interact together naturally. We could say that our daily routine requires thinking that is an interplay of the two. Traditional schools have emphasized comprehension more than apprehension. John Dewey, a pioneer of educational psychology, says, "When intellectual experience and its material are taken to be primary, the cord that binds nature and experience is cut."

Exercise

Think back on your formal education. Which of the two following columns was emphasized?

Comprehension	Apprehension
Knowledge from Theory	Internal Understanding
Words and Language	Art and Visuals
Thinking	Sensing, Feeling
Describing Ideas	Exploring Ideas
Analyzing	Synthesizing
Parts	Wholes
Defending	Discovering
Theorizing	Experimenting

Carefully planned active learning experiences, as described in detail in chapter 5 and the examples in chapter 6–10, are primarily designed to stimulate the apprehension process of learning. Remember, *one process should not be emphasized over the other.* The two should keep balance with each other.

One definition of a teacher is someone who stimulates thinking in order to achieve learning. Dr. Leah M. Serck, a professor of education at Concordia University, Seward, Nebraska, stimulated my thinking. I was a senior majoring in theology when Dr. Serck led a "teaching laboratory." She designed a workshop on the story of creation, using learning centers. All of the centers involved active learning. I immediately thought how wonderful this approach would be for children. In the centers students created songs, dramas, murals, and sculptures. Each of our groups reported back to the class showing our "work." Suddenly a wonderful moment of truth found me. As if throwing a switch, all the theological studies and discussions of Genesis made sense to me. Somewhere in the play dough, in the new songs, in the colored scarfs floating in the air, the Holy Spirit whispered, "This is what the words in Genesis mean." There is no age limit for active learning.

Retention
Methods of Learning

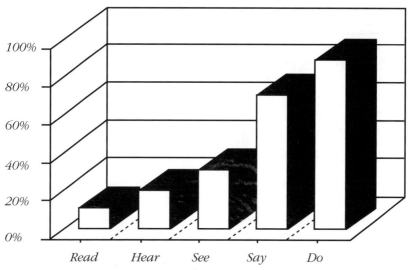

The graph above demonstrates the degrees of abstraction required for learning events. The theory of the model suggests that the best learning experience builds from the bottom up; a successful "do" experience involves several of the lower building blocks: read, hear, see, and say. Consider the following scenarios:

A student in class hears the teacher say, "God is merciful. He forgives us." The student hears a description of God's action.

The repentant child receives a hug form her parent who says, "It saddens me that you broke the lamp. God loves you, and I love you. God forgives you, and so do I."

Which do you think is likely to be more effective?
Chances are, the second example will be more effective because it allows the child to experience God's love in action.

Intentional active learning gives the classroom teacher opportunities to be real and in touch with students.

<INDUCTIVE AND DEDUCTIVE> TEACHING

Deductive teaching is often related to comprehension. Inductive teaching is often related to apprehension.
Inductive teaching involves reasoning from a part to a whole, from the specific to the general.<
Deductive teaching involves reaching a conclusion by reasoning from the general to the specific.>
Examine this diamond lesson:

Beginning with inductive style the teacher announces, "Today we are going to learn about mercy. Mercy is the willingness to forgive." The learners are then encouraged to share anything they know about mercy. They might be asked, "Where have you heard the word before?" The teacher encourages divergence—allowing the discussion to progress in multiple directions. Leaps of abstraction are celebrated. The teacher might say, "Mercy spelled backwards is ycrem, what kind of a feeling do you get when you hear that word?" or "What do you see happening when there is lots of ycrem?"

The teacher could ask if any would be willing to tell about a time when they were forgiven.

Then move to the Bible story, "Let me tell you a story that I call *The Forgiving Father,*" the teacher says as she reads the Luke account of the prodigal son. "Close your eyes and imagine you are the son in this story as I read this ending,

> *So he got up and went to his father. But while he was still a long way off, his father saw him and was filled with compassion for him; he ran to his son, threw his arms around him and kissed him.*

The son said to him, "Father, I have sinned against heaven and against you. I am no longer worthy to be called your son."

But the father said to his servants, "Quick! Bring the best robe and put it on him. Put a ring on his finger and sandals on his feet. Bring the fattened calf and kill it. Let's have a feast and celebrate. For this son of mine was dead and is alive again; he was lost and is found!" So they began to celebrate. (Luke 15:20–24)

After the story is told, a group of students act it out as the teacher retells the Bible story. Then the teacher writes everyone's response to the question "What did you think of when you saw that roleplay?"

When the concept has been taken to the widest abstraction, or when half the time is up, the teacher facilitates the process of gathering all the thoughts and ideas together; she begins the deductive style. As in sifting for gold, the ideas start taking narrower and narrower focus. The thoughts, themes, truths, and trends are distilled and synthesized until a single statement of truth is articulated.

The teacher could ask the following sequence of questions:

"Look at the thoughts on the list we made. Think about feelings you had when I read the Bible story and from everything we said thus far. What themes have been repeated? I'll write your thoughts on the board too."

"What truth do these themes have in common?"

"What title would you give to all these truths?"

"Would you all agree that this is the central truth for today's lesson?"

The diamond is complete. The teacher could pray this closing prayer, "Thank You, Holy Spirit, for teaching us that our heavenly Father is a God of mercy. Amen."

The balance of induction and deduction helps children see and fill their minds with truth. Good teaching has balance because thoughts without content are empty, and intuitions without concepts are blind.

Exercise

Examine the inductive and deductive activities in a class session. Tape yourself or get permission to tape someone else. Replay the tape and record the amount of time the teacher speaks and the amount of time everyone else speaks. (It's great if you have a stopwatch.) Inductive activities usually have much less teacher talk than deductive activities.

Look at the graph on the next page. It depicts how many words per minute are being processed. There is a big gap (about 300 words) between the spoken word of the teacher and the thoughts of the student. During a well-planned inductive activity the thoughts tend to relate to the activity, while minds often wander during a deductive activity. Teachers might want to speak less in order to teach more.

Words Per Minute
average

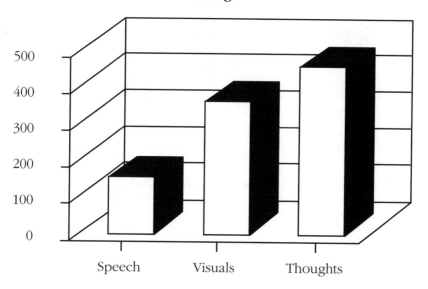

Speech   Visuals   Thoughts

Reference

Kolb, David A., *Experiential Learning: Experience as the Source of Learning ad Development.* Englewood Cliffs, NJ: Prentice Hall, Inc., 1984.

The Learner

Then [Jesus] said to them, "Whoever welcomes this little child in My name welcomes Me; and whoever welcomes Me welcomes the one who sent Me. For he who is least among you all—he is the greatest." (Luke 9:48)

The best learning experiences consider characteristics of the learners—who they are. Learning activities need to be a good "fit" with the needs and learning abilities of the children, youth, or adults. Effective use of active learning does not require a complete understanding of all the developmental issues of children's psychology, sociology, and theology. However, we may embrace active learning methods with more enthusiasm when we understand that these methods are embedded in sound theory and we know how we can use these methods to educate the whole child.

Most teachers find that they use active learning strategies more readily when they teach from published lessons that have been developed for the specific age and spiritual maturity level. Teachers, then, observe their learners and adapt the resources to fit their situations.

TEACHING THE LEARNER—THE WHOLE LEARNER

Teachers expand their knowledge of children as they study educational theory and observation. They then learn the world of a child by carefully watching and listening to them. The world of a child or teenager is so different from the world of an adult. And although adults have some memories of their own childhood, they can no longer appreciate how a child thinks and feels. Adults are foreigners in a child's world.

This chapter will help you become familiar with your students. Your preparation can help you better respond to how they think and feel and where their interests are. As we gain teaching experience, we reflect on our many classroom failures and successes. As we grow, we become increasingly aware of why our children behave the way they do. We not only know the right things to do, but we also understand why we do them.

In this chapter we explore the learner—the whole learner. Our ability to design useful active learning experiences grows as we become more aware of basic differences in age and faith development. We will review theories of the whole child focused on the following topics:

Spiritual needs of children

Intellectual and moral development

Left and right brain dominance

Preferred learning styles

AN OLD CONCEPT

Down through the ages, good educators have looked at things as integrated wholes. The writings of Moses include a view of faith in God that involves the whole person. Jesus affirms the concept further.

> *[A teacher of the law asked Jesus,] "Of all the commandments, which is the most important?"*
>
> *"The most important one," answered Jesus, "is this: 'Hear, O Israel, the Lord our God, the Lord is one. Love the Lord your God with all your heart and with all your soul and with all your mind and with all your strength.' "* (Mark 12:28b–30)

Jesus mentions the heart, soul, mind, and strength. Love for God was isolated neither to the spiritual nor to the intellectual or physical realms. Love for God encompasses our entire existence. Teaching the faith also encompasses the whole person.

Exercise

A mind map can help you see a child as a whole person. Like the mind map in the introduction of this book, you can make a mind map of a child in your classroom. Draw a mind map similar to the sample on the next page. Write the name of a specific child in the center. In the surrounding bubbles write the major influences that make up his or her world. Then branch out beyond that and consider all the extended parts of the child's world. Include yourself in the map so you have a sense of your connectedness to the child.

Your Mind Map of a Child

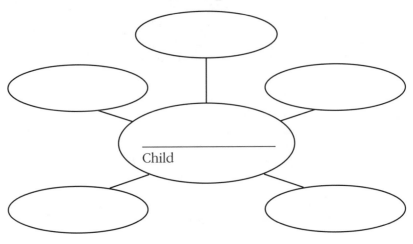

Child

THE SPIRITUAL NEEDS OF CHILDREN

Spiritual growth involves our understanding of God's will and our response to His love. God causes this growth to take place through the Gospel. While spiritual growth can take massive leaps, it ordinarily occurs in an orderly fashion. We can observe certain stages or levels in the spiritual maturity of children.

Spiritual growth does not happen automatically. As a matter of fact, our natural sinful condition does not want Christ-centered growth to occur at all. The sinful nature shows itself in pride, self-love, and self-will—all obstacles to the spiritual growth of a Christian.

Most children in classrooms that share the love of Jesus also possess another nature; they are "new creations" whose new, spiritual natures fight against their sinful natures. God works actively in them to give them the desire and power to grow in their responses to His love.

Spiritual development is an ongoing development that permeates every phase of a child's life; it does not occur only in formal settings, like a Sunday school class. As they continue in God's Word, children who hear the Gospel continue to receive God's power for spiritual growth after they walk out of the classroom door. In addition to remembering the messages they heard, children experience God's love as Christian family and friends live the Gospel in helping to fulfill the following needs in the students' lives:

> to be loved and to love
>
> to be secure and safe
>
> to feel safe when exploring the unknown
>
> to be a responsible member of a family
>
> to have time and space to be alone
>
> to learn skills for making friends
>
> to learn to trust adults
>
> to be accepted for who they are and to be forgiven
>
> to achieve and to serve
>
> to find joy in the fellowship of others

Note that most of these important needs cannot be fulfilled only in the classroom. The family environment provides the primary arena for the development of these qualities. Teachers can, however, have a significant effect when they respond consistently, dramatically, and repeatedly with love and concern. Children need significant adults other than their parents to reinforce their self-esteem. Teachers can also become a support system for the family. The role of others, such as teachers, becomes especially important to children of dysfunctional families. God continues to work in remarkable ways to care for His children—often through the efforts of Christian teachers He brings into their lives.

HOW CHILDREN DEVELOP INTELLECTUALLY AND MORALLY—PIAGET AND KOHLBERG

All children have one thing in common: They differ from one another. Yet some characteristics are common to all children as they grow and develop.

Jean Piaget describes the child's intellectual development in four age-related stages. The stages differ; yet they build upon each other.

Lawrence Kohlberg went a step beyond Piaget when he studied stages of moral reasoning. The chart that follows summarizes the theories of Piaget and Kohlberg. Note the similarities and the implications for teaching the faith. Kohlberg's three levels correspond to stages 2 through 4 of Piaget.

Piaget	Intellectually	Kohlberg	Morally
Stage 1: SENSORIMOTOR (birth to age 2)	The child is largely engaged in countless physical transactions as he experiments with his environment.		
Stage 2: PRE-OPERATIONAL THOUGHT (age 2 to 7)	The child is basically egocentric. He gradually becomes more social in his behavior. He begins to make judgments in terms of how things look to him. "Why" questions are characteristic at this stage.	Level 1 PRE-CONVENTIONAL	The child is primarily concerned for consequences to self. The child is afraid of punishment and whether an action is good or bad. Because much of this is discovery, the child confirms what is "bad" by the reaction of adults in their life.

Piaget	Intellectually	Kohlberg	Morally
Stage 3: CONCRETE OPERATIONS (age 7 to ll)	The child begins to show some logic in her thinking and conclusions. She plays games involving rules more easily. She can think about parts and wholes independently of each other.	Level 2 CONVENTIONAL LEVEL	The child is concerned for meeting social expectations. Children are orientated toward the approval of others who are close to them. The child begins to give in to the will of others, even if she suffers for it. She is more afraid of doing harm than being fearful of punishment.
Stage 4: FORMAL THINKING (beginning with age 12)	During these years he completes the move from concrete operations to hypothetical and deductive reasoning.	Level 3 PRINCIPLE LEVEL	The older teenager or adult develops a concern for fidelity to self-chosen principles. Persons have an orientation toward moral principles that have universal validity. They see how law grows out of principles, not vice versa. The person is ready to stand alone in order to live as he believes. Truth is not controlled by one's own group: Mankind is the community and justice is the goal for all.

KNOW YOUR STUDENTS

In *Go and Make Disciples* (CPH, 1992) Jane Fryar reviews the theories of Piaget, Kohlberg, and other developmental psychologists. She concludes:

Know your students. Ultimately that is the message developmental psychologists have to share with us. And it is an important message, a crucial message in fact. We must know our students, know them as individuals. As we disciple the children or young people our Lord has placed in our classrooms, we can assume that

- *each student is in a different place along the road in his or her personal walk with Jesus Christ;*
- *each student is at a different place in his or her ability to think through and reason about moral decisions and spiritual questions;*
- *each student has different personal needs and hurts;*
- *each student has different strengths of character and hopes for the future given by God Himself;*
- *each student has a different learning style and unique intellectual potential.*

Because this is so, a teacher who assumes that each student in a particular first-grade classroom reasons and acts at Kohlberg's moral stage 1 or who believes that all the students in a given seventh-grade classroom will reason and act at Kohlberg's moral stage 3 will without any doubt miss opportunities to nurture his students' relationship with Jesus Christ.

Christian teachers will often find the insights of developmental psychologists helpful, a good gift from the Creator who allows His creatures to explore the richness of His creation. At the same time, we cannot overlook our need to get to know individual students. Where do they struggle with understanding the Christian faith? with applying it? For what hurts do they need Christ's comfort? With what sins do they need to be lovingly, but firmly confronted? With what causes for celebration has God gifted them, and how can we join and encourage them in that celebration? (Go and Make Disciples, *pages 148–49. All rights reserved.)*

TEACHING THE LEARNER—ALL THE LEARNERS

But eagerly desire the greater gifts. And now I will show you the most excellent way. (1 Corinthians 12:31)

BRAIN HEMISPHERISITY AND LEARNING STYLES

Just as children learn differently in different stages of development, they learn in ways that differ from one another. Perhaps this difference can best be explained by recent studies of the brain. The cerebrum, which makes up two-thirds of the human brain, is divided into left and right hemispheres.

Left Brain: The left side of the brain is the thinking side. It handles the linear, logical, analytical, and intellectual functions. Speaking, reading, and writing happen on the left side.

Right Brain: The right side of the brain is the intuitive side. This side "thinks" holistically. It is emotional, dramatic, imaginative, and random.

People develop a hemispheric dominance. That is, they prefer to operate out of one side more than the other. This dominance, or preference, accounts for the differences in personality and learning. After kindergarten most traditional education does not value the right brain learner. Right brain thinking is neglected and sometimes even discouraged. This is fortunate for the left brain students, because they are able to get good grades and feel secure with the education process. But this frustrates right brain learners because they are not given an even chance to demonstrate their intelligence. Instead, the right brained learner is made to feel like a square peg in a round hole.

The Bible does not discuss brain hemispherisity. Note, however, the way St. Paul describes the differing spiritual gifts. (While spiritual gifts involve more than natural abilities, many of the differing gifts do suggest differences in the talents God has given to various individuals.)

Now you are the body of Christ, and each one of you is a part of it. And in the church God has appointed first of all apostles, second prophets, third teachers, then workers of miracles, also those having gifts of healing, those able to help others, those with gifts of administration, and those speaking in different kinds of tongues. Are all apostles? Are all prophets? Are all teachers? Do all work miracles? Do all have gifts of healing? Do all speak in tongues? Do all interpret? But eagerly desire the greater gifts. And now I will show you the most excellent way. (1 Corinthians 12:27–31)

In 1 Corinthians 13 Paul discusses "the most excellent way"— the way is love. God gives this gift to all Christians, children and teachers alike. In a Christian classroom love permeates everything we do, whether students are active or passive. Part of a teacher's love is the desire to nurture our students—all the students.

Exercise

Which set of words best describes you?

Open	**Gentle**
Talkative	**Amiable**
Playful	**Kind**
Outgoing	**Peaceful**
Bold	**Exacting**
Adventurous	**Precise**
Daring	**Orderly**
Assertive	**Clear Thinker**

Now think of the students you teach. If you have 19 students in your class, you have 19 different personalities. Very likely they will not all fall into the same section of the chart. For example, your class may have one student who is open, talkative, playful, and outgoing, and another who is exacting, precise, orderly, and a clear thinker. Another may have characteristics of more than one section, perhaps gentle, talkative, kind, and peaceful. When you use both passive and active teaching styles, you increase the likelihood of reaching all your students.

Most people fall into one or two of these four basic personality groups. A closer look at the horizontal and vertical lines on the chart can help you analyze the individuals in your classes.

A horizontal axis represents how people take in information—how they perceive data.

DOING ———————————————————— **WATCHING**

On the left you have those who use active experimentation, or doing.

On the right you have people who take in the data—reflective observation, or watching.

A vertical axis represents a continuum of how people process information, how they make sense of what they have taken in.

FEELING

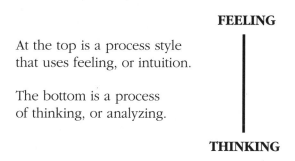

At the top is a process style that uses feeling, or intuition.

The bottom is a process of thinking, or analyzing.

THINKING

When you put the horizontal and vertical axes together, you can describe the four basic types of personalities.

Doing Feeler	Watching Feeler
Doing Thinker	Watching Thinker

Each student is unique. However, we can make some generalizations about those with each type of personality

Watching/Feeler (23.4 percent of the population)

Watching/feeling students are delightful because they care about others. They also learn best in a group setting. They are creative and social. Watching/feelers like to ask *why* questions. They have a need for cooperation and acceptance. They value personal relationships, helping others, and being liked. They are friendly, supportive, respectful, willing, dependable, and agreeable. They use opinions and stories rather than facts and data.

Watching/feeling students love active learning because they can interact with others.

Watching/Thinker (30.8 percent of the population)

Watching/thinker students are wonderful because they think things through. They like to ask *what* questions. They are most concerned with being organized—having all the facts and being careful before taking action. They need to be accurate. Watching/thinkers are comfortable in positions in which they can check facts and figures and be sure they are right. The watcher/thinker wants to learn and to decide.

Watching/thinker students do not like the initial steps of active learning because they are not best suited for active engagement.

However, they can help the class as you reflect upon the experience and analyze the meaning.

Doing/Thinker (17.5 percent of the population)

Doing/thinker students are exciting because they like results. They can put ideas into action. Doing/thinkers likes to ask *how does it work* kinds of questions. They tend to speak and act quickly. Doing/thinkers are comfortable being class leaders. They like action and motion. Learning is best if they can use it.

For obvious reasons, doing/thinker students love active learning.

Doing/Feeler (28.2 percent of the population)

Doing/feeler students are fascinating because they are so imaginative. They love innovation and application of ideas to new situations. They like to ask *what if* questions. They are sociable, stimulating, enthusiastic and are good at involving and motivating others. Doing/feelers focus on people rather than on tasks. They use opinions and stories rather than facts and data. Doing/feeler students love active learning because they utilize both their perception skills and process skills.

When we teach in a passive style, we only honor the watching/thinker students. A combination of active and passive styles will more likely provide the balance that will benefit the majority of students in a class.

References:

Duska, R. and Wheland, M. *Moral Development: A Guide to Piaget and Kohlberg*. New York: Paulist Press, 1975.

Fritz, Dorothy. *The Spiritual Growth of Children*. Philadelphia: Westminster Press, 1957.

McCarthy, Bernice. *The 4MAT System, Teaching to Learning Styles with Right/Left Mode Techniques*. Barrington, IL: Excel, Inc., 1987.

GET ACTIVE

Schacter, Daniel L. *Searching for Memory, the Brain, the Mind, and the Past.* New York: Basic Books, 1996.

Wadsworth, Barry J. *Piaget for the Classroom Teacher.* New York: Longman Inc., 1978.

Wycoff, Joyce. *Mindmapping.* New York: Berkley, 1991.

Teacher Readiness

Who is wise and understanding among you? Let him show it by his good life, by deeds done in the humility that comes from wisdom. (James 3:13)

Note that active learning engages the whole learner—mind, heart, and spirit—in a discovery process. Are you ready to use the methods of active learning in your classroom? If those who provided *your* educational experiences relied primarily on passive methods, you may need to change some of the ways you think about teaching and learning. Unfortunately, the axiom "We teach the way we were taught" is true for many individuals.

By now it should be clear that effective teaching is a balance of both active and passive teaching styles. Balance, however, is not widely practiced. Some advocates of active learning fail to achieve that balance because they minimize the value of any passive methods. Many readers, however, may find it challenging to achieve this balance because of their experiences with passive methods. This "teacher-centered" paradigm has become a part of much of our culture. Has this been your experience? In this chapter we seek to encourage and support you as you attempt a change in your teaching style. Change may not come easily. It is not a matter of age. For most, it is a matter of thinking "outside the box."

Exercise

Analyze your own experience. How were you taught? In the three boxes below, draw what you remember of your formal schooling. Do not attempt to create an accurate drawing; for this activity we simply want you to use your right brain to explore your memories through shapes and sketching. Think of a specific classroom for each of the categories below.

Early Schooling (grade 3 or younger)	Middle Years of School (grades 4–8)	Most Recent Schooling (above grade 8)

Look at the drawings and reflect upon what you see.

What recollections are most vivid?

What similarities and differences, if any, do you note as you recall your education experiences?

What pattern, if any, do you see?

While the difference between conformity to a good idea and remaining in an old rut may be difficult to determine, we would agree on the value of uniformity. Railroads tracks, for example, need uniformity. All trains run on parallel tracks that are 4 feet, 8½ inches apart. Because of that uniformity, trains and tracks are interchangeable all across the United States and even across Europe. Did you ever stop and wonder why that exact distance between tracks was chosen? Perhaps the spacing of the tracks goes back to Europe, where the ruts in the road made by wagons were approximately 4 feet, 8½ inches across. This spacing of wagon wheels also happens to be the same as that of the wheels on Roman chariots dating back to Caesar and the time of Christ. It seems that the chariot makers discovered 4 feet, 8½ inches as the perfect space between wheels following a team of two horses. Is the uniformity between chariot, wagon, and railroad track spacing conformity or is that a rut?

What teaching ruts (if any) have you adopted?

You need to make a change if you use nothing but active learning methods. Likewise, you need to make a change if you use nothing but passive learning methods. Change is not easy; logic alone will not convince you. Once a practice has been established, it is hard to imagine anything else. It is easy to stay in a rut.

OVERUSE OF A STRENGTH IS A WEAKNESS

Many teachers overuse their teaching strength. It's not just too much of a good thing, it's too much of the same thing. Teaching the way we like to learn is comfortable for us because we are going with our strength. Some children—those like you—will do well. However, the other children (maybe more than two-thirds of your class) will not do as well as they might if a variety of teaching methods were used.

Try this simple exercise: Fold your arms. Keep them crossed for a moment sensing how your body feels as you have your arms crossed. Look at your hands. Which hand is under your arm and which is outside your arm?

Now fold your arms the opposite way, with a different hand under your arm and a different hand on top. This might take a bit of practice until you actually have the opposite position. Hold them in this position for a while. How does this position feel?

When you first folded you arms your "preferred" way, you did not have to think about how to accomplish the task. It felt natural, even comfortable. Unless you have a very good reason for doing otherwise, you will probably always fold your arms in this way.

Now transfer this experience to teaching. Everyone has preferences or habits in the way they teach. Habits are hard to change. You probably agree that it will take more than logic to convince you to try other styles of teaching. You will have to go through an awkward and uncomfortable stage called learning. As you work through that stage, think about the potential blessings to your students when they experience balanced learning activities. And, remember the opportunities God is giving you in your classroom.

FEED AND TEND THE LAMBS AND SHEEP

God gives teachers an important calling. He also provides the power to carry out the tasks He gives us. At times we will fail Him. But Jesus has earned our forgiveness. As we come again to receive the power He gives us in His Word, Baptism, and the Lord's Supper, God invites us to begin anew, learning from our mistakes and growing in our abilities as teachers of the Good News.

As you think about your opportunities to explore more effective ways to feed and tend the lambs and sheep, think about Simon Peter. He seems to have been a doing/feeler. His personality type got him into some tight situations. Yet, Jesus' message is clear, *I want you, Simon son of John, to be a shepherd.*

When they had finished eating, Jesus said to Simon Peter, "Simon son of John, do you love Me more than these?"

"Yes, Lord," he said, "You know that I love You."

Jesus said, "Feed My lambs."

Again Jesus said, "Simon son of John, do you truly love Me?"

He answered, "Yes, Lord, You know that I love You."

Jesus said, "Take care of My sheep."

The third time He said to him, "Simon son of John, do you love Me?"

Peter was hurt because Jesus asked him the third time, "Do you love Me?" He said, "Lord, You know all things; You know that I love You."

Jesus said, "Feed My sheep." (John 21:15–17)

Of course, not all of Jesus' followers were doing/feelers. Perhaps John was a watching/feeler, and Martha may have been a doing/thinker. You may be more like one of them.

Whatever personality you have, teaching the faith can be a rich and rewarding task. Jane Fryar says it this way:

You play an active, important part in the transformation process God has initiated in the lives of your students, the process of discipleship. You make it possible for that process to happen more thoroughly and more quickly that it would without you. (Changing Hearts, Changing Lives: Practical Ideas to Make a Difference in Your Classroom, *by Jane L. Fryar. CPH, 1996, page 24.)*

Teaching the faith is more an art than a science. Paint with joy. Color with hope and sculpt with faith. By God's power His Spirit will transform your teaching with powerful effects that transcend the confines of your classroom.

Active Learning

[Speaking to Nicodemus, Jesus said,] "The wind blows wherever it pleases. You hear its sound, but you cannot tell where it comes from or where it is going. So it is with everyone born of the Spirit." (John 3:8)

Active learning involves the whole person in the learning process.

Active learning centers on the learner, not the teacher.

Active learning is complex; it requires both knowledge and skill to facilitate.

Active learning is fun and serious.

Active learning is complex; it requires both knowledge and skill to facilitate.

Active learning is fun and serious.

Active learning is a highly effective tool for teaching the faith.

Active learning is the most widely used learning technique in the world—except in classrooms.

ACTIVE LEARNING—NOT JUST FUN AND GAMES

The following model depicts the complete cycle of active learning. Without steps 2–4 learning is left to chance. Then active learning would become no more than fun and games. The processing and connecting steps help students focus their ideas. Step 4 projects the learning into everyday life.

ACTIVE LEARNING MODEL

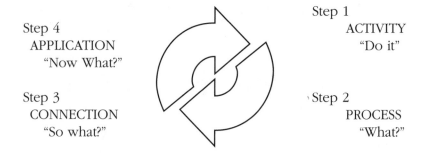

Step 4
APPLICATION
"Now What?"

Step 1
ACTIVITY
"Do it"

Step 3
CONNECTION
"So what?"

Step 2
PROCESS
"What?"

All the active learning experiences in this book are built upon this model. The sequence is a process that includes elements of both sides of the brain and honors all learning styles. Teachers of younger children will need to focus on steps 1 and 2. These children have not yet developed concrete operations (stage 3 of Piaget). For them, steps 3 and 4 are more teacher centered. The teacher tells the story and tells children how it is applied. We will discuss these steps in detail in chapter 6. For other learners all the following steps apply.

Step 1	Activity	("Do It")

We begin the active learning process with a step that leads the students through a structured activity that involves everyone in action or interaction. Many things can be used as the activity including real life experiences.

Activities may include and are not limited to the following:
- field trips
- service projects
- class projects
- debates
- obstacle courses
- dramas
- song writing
- roleplays
- games
- building or creating structures
- creative writing
- dance
- simulation games
- rhythm and music activities

The teacher introduces the activity and explains all the rules. Sometimes the teacher may announce the topic. However, he or she avoids suggesting what the students are expected to learn from the activity. The teacher does, however, clearly establish rules and boundaries. Then the teacher monitors the activity, participating only to enhance the experience.

Step 2	Process	("What?")

Immediately following the activity, the teacher instructs the students to reflect upon what happened. Individuals may write about their experience, for example. Or, they may respond to questions such as: *What happened? What did you see? What were you aware of? What did you feel? What were your thoughts about the others and about yourself? Did you have any surprises?*

This inductive process continues, including all the thoughts and perspectives. The teacher or breakout groups post all the comments on a list. Everything becomes important data for consideration. By accepting all observations as valuable and important, the teacher encourages participation. At this point there are no right and wrong answers; the teacher is simply gathering information about how students think and feel. He or she could simply go around the room asking each student for his or her reaction and then write it on the chalkboard. Every comment is recorded exactly as said, even if some repeat comments made earlier.

Once you have collected all the data and brainstormed all observable possibilities, you are ready for the next step.

| **Step 3** | **Connection** | **("So What?")** |

This is the pivotal step in active learning. The teacher asks the students to look at all the collected data and consider what connections they observe. The teacher is now shaping and drawing out collaboration. Through this process the class is synthesizing the information. As in the previous step, the comments and observations of the students are written down. Writing student comments for all to see can work powerfully to keep the focus on the students rather than on the teacher. Younger children, even prereading students, also respond well to this technique.

The teacher leads the discussion with one to three of the following open-ended questions:

Do you see any trends in what we wrote?

What is true about all these thoughts we had?

What seem to be some common themes in our experience?

How might you summarize our statements?

What could you say about the variety of our comments?

Do you hear and see any connections to our Bible story?

How does this connect to what you know about the teachings of Jesus?

What, if anything, disagrees with how you think and feel?

The teacher looks for ways to connect the students' thoughts and feelings to the point of the lesson. In addition to learning the point of the lesson, students may glean more (or something different) than the teacher expects. Keep the focus on the learner.

| **Step 4** | **Application** | **("Now What?")** |

What did you learn today and how will you be different because of what you have learned? This question provides the focus of this wrap-up discussion. Children can write, draw, or verbally explain what they learned and how they will be different because of the learning. The application directs students outside the classroom and into the future. At this time the teacher also can encourage and guide. "Based on what you have discussed today," the teacher might conclude, "what real and significant changes might be made in your life?" Remember, the Gospel at work in the lesson motivates and empowers real changes. Teachers can use commitment cards, letters of intent, poetry, "to do" lists, and setting goals to reinforce the learning and give it direction into real life.

Another effective process is to incorporate a closing ceremony to bring closure to learning time. Circle prayers, candle lighting, and singing are familiar worship activities. Worship can bring learning to a conclusion with a sense of transcendence and purpose. Ultimately, we want Christian learning to move to faith-filled action in the lives of students who know, understand, and do God's will.

SHIFTING ROLES

You can see from the steps described that the roles of the student and teacher change. This shifting balance is delicate and requires skillful facilitation from the teacher.

	Teacher Role	Student Role	Objective
Activity (Step 1)	Set up the activity and manage boundaries	The center of attention. Totally involved in the experience and fully engaged in the moment.	Students participate fully in the activity, demonstrating awareness of what is happening.
Process (Step 2)	Lead the collection of data. Facilitate the discussion of the students, but do not add own thoughts.	Make observations and tell the truth as they have experienced it. Listen to the other students.	Students share all their thoughts and ideas concerning the activity.
Connection (Step 3) Application	First, collect all the connections the students make to life and the faith. Draw upon the students' comments and connect the learning. Next, and only if the students don't "get" it, make observations that teach the faith.	Students draw upon their process discussion to synthesize the learning. They listen and consider the teacher's input.	Students connect the experience to the truths and teachings of the faith.

	Teacher Role	Student Role	Objective
Application (Step 4)	The teacher actively encourages and solicits commitment from the students to act upon the learning. The teacher leads in worship and prayer that moves the learning into action.	Students build upon the learning and explore ways to act on what they have learned. They participate in experiences that dramatize action. They reflect upon the teacher's input about change and action.	Students connect the truths and teachings of the faith to their life. They make a plan and a commitment to change.

THE MASTER TEACHER

We call Jesus the Master Teacher and recognize His all-knowing wisdom. He demonstrated this wisdom when He taught of things unseen and things beyond belief with clarity and action. His "students," the disciples, were often clueless concerning the kingdom of God so Jesus instructed them in ways they could comprehend and remember. Let's apply the active learning model to the account of the Last Supper in the Upper Room (John 13:1–17).

It was just before the Passover Feast. Jesus knew that the time had come for Him to leave this world and go to the Father. Having loved His own who were in the world, He now showed the full extent of His love.

The evening meal was being served, and the devil had already prompted Judas Iscariot, son of Simon, to betray Jesus. Jesus knew that the Father had put all things under His power, and that He had come from God and was returning to God. (vv. 1–3)

Step 1   **Activity**   **("Do It")**

So He got up from the meal, took off His outer clothing, and wrapped a towel around His waist. After that, He poured water into a basin and began to wash His disciples' feet, drying them with the towel that was wrapped around Him.

He came to Simon Peter, who said to Him, "Lord, are You going to wash my feet?"

Jesus replied, "You do not know now what I am doing, but later you will understand."

"No," said Peter, "You shall never wash my feet."

Jesus answered, "Unless I wash you, you have no part with Me."

"Then, Lord," Simon Peter replied, "not just my feet but my hands and my head as well!"

Jesus answered, "A person who has had a bath needs only to wash his feet; his whole body is clean. And you are clean, though not every one of you." For He knew who was going to betray Him, and that was why He said not every one was clean. (vv. 4–10)

Step 2   **Process**   **("What?")**

When He had finished washing their feet, He put on His clothes and returned to His place. "Do you understand what I have done for you?" He asked them. (v. 12)

Step 3   **Connection**   **("So What?")**

"You call Me 'Teacher' and 'Lord,' and rightly so, for that is what I am. Now that I, your Lord and Teacher, have washed your feet, you also should wash one another's feet." (vv. 13–14)

Step 4   **Application**   **("Now What?")**

I have set you an example that you should do as I have done for you. I tell you the truth, no servant is greater than his master, nor is a messenger greater than the one who sent him. Now that you know these things, you will be blessed if you do them. (vv. 15–17)

We see active learning over and over again in the ministry of Jesus. Jesus found teachable moments in all of life. Active learning brings life—and its teachable moments—into the classroom. Push back the desks and imagine creating moments of life that can bring the story of salvation alive. To a large degree, effective teaching begins with you, it depends upon the Spirit, and it celebrates love in action.

"WILL ACTIVE LEARNING WORK FOR *ME*, IN *MY* CLASSROOM?'

If the concept of active learning is new for you, the idea of using these strategies may scare you. Consider the following:

Effective Active Learning Requires Careful Planning

While much learning does occur even without careful planning, you cannot count on it. Most Christian education settings provide only a limited amount of time to achieve the desired outcomes. Therefore you, as the teacher, will want to plan activities that use the time effectively.

The four-step process provides a framework on which to build effective active learning experiences. As you examine the various activities presented, the nature of the activity and setting, and the development of the learner influence what happens in each step.

Active Learning Tends to Be Effective

First and foremost, the Gospel tells us who Jesus is (the Savior) and what He teaches (the way of salvation). As the writers tell The Story, they also give us a glimpse of the educational methodology Jesus followed. Jesus could have used passive methods to teach about servanthood and about His power; at times He did. But imagine the impact Jesus' message had in the account above and when the disciples were afraid they would drown (Luke 8:22–25).

Active Learning Capitalizes on Teachable Moments

On Easter Day Jesus appeared to two disciples who did not know He had risen from the dead and did not recognize Him (Luke 24:13–35). At that moment they were very aware of all that had happened on Maundy Thursday and Good Friday. After giving these disciples an opportunity to tell what they knew (vv. 17–24; activity and process), Jesus explained the teachings of the Old Testament that these disciples previously could not have understood so completely (vv. 25–35; connection and application). Jesus' timing was excellent. His death and resurrection provided an optimal time to explain to His disciples what the Scriptures teach about God's plan of salvation through Christ Jesus.

When we plan most active learning experiences, we are attempting to develop teachable moments in our classrooms. However, effective teaching will also go beyond formal class time. Some of our most effective teaching will occur—by the power of the Spirit—when we develop an activity "on the spot" in response to a teachable moment that occurs in our classrooms.

Active Learning Does Require Special Attention to Classroom Behavior

Active learning involves *activity*. When children engage in activities with others, they sometimes get noisy or jostle one another. For those reasons you may be tempted to avoid such activities. As you ponder this issue, consider the following:

> Noise and movement often contribute to learning. You need to develop standards for "good" noise and movement. Then monitor those conditions accordingly.

> Children frequently misbehave in passive situations also. Sometimes that misbehavior is not as noisy—and therefore not as noticeable to other adults—as the misbehavior can be in more active situations. Teachers sometimes work to the detriment of learning in order to prevent noise that will cause other adults to judge them to be poor teachers.

Active learning experiences motivate most children. As a result, their behavior will improve.

Not every class will respond the same way to an activity. Therefore you will need to tailor your activities to your situations. For example, one type of activity may involve children standing near signs posted at various places in their room to tell if they strongly agree, agree, disagree, or strongly disagree with statement you are reading. If your class does not respond well to such movement, you could have them stay at their chairs and respond by sitting, crouching, standing, and standing with hands raised.

Thus, active learning involves attention to details of classroom management. With no planning and no attention to such details, you may achieve bedlam instead of active learning. But with planning and attention to details you may provide experiences in which, by the power of the Spirit, learning occurs as it never has before.

Make photocopies of the following page to use for planning your own active learning experiences.

Reference:

Pfeiffer, J. W. and Ballwe, A. C. *Using Structured Experiences in Human Resource Development*. San Diego: University Associates, 1988.

GET ACTIVE

	Teacher Role	Student Role	Objective
Activity (Step 1)			
Process (Step 2)			
Connection (Step 3)			
Application (Step 4)			

Active Learning Designs: Early Childhood

[Jesus] replied, "Blessed rather are those who hear the word of God and obey it." (Luke 11:28)

The early childhood level has led the way in active learning. Early childhood educators know that children in the preoperational thought stage (Piaget) learn primarily through sensory awareness activities. The world literally takes "shape" in young children as they touch, smell, taste, look at, and listen to things around them. They are the most typical example of active learner and, in fact, would be stunted in their growth without activity. Note how CPH's Early

Childhood level of the Our Life in Christ Sunday school curriculum reflects these ideas:

> *Instead of expecting children to learn the way adults do—by sitting, listening, and discussing—let's teach the way they learn best—by being actively involved in the learning process. Let's make the Sunday school classroom a place and experience where children become involved in learning about our wonderful God and what He did for us through the saving work of His Son, Jesus Christ. ... Centers help children learn in multisensory ways. They help children experience new things and grow through their experiences.* (Plus Pages: Ideas for Activity Centers, *Preschool, Fall 1997, ©CPH 1997, page 3. All rights reserved.*)

With preschool children the active learning model follows the first two steps in the same way as other age levels. During Steps 3 and 4 the teacher leads the children into connections and applications. The teacher builds vocabulary and tells the story of God. The teacher points out how biblical truths apply to children's lives. The teacher is fully aware that the "talking and telling" does not focus on comprehension of the concepts; rather, the teacher introduces faith talk and relationship building.

> *You (the teacher) are the bridge, the link that connects what they are doing at a center with what God is doing in their lives, and with what they will hear later during the presentation of the Bible story. You are bringing God into their everyday lives in a very real way. ... You are building a relationship with them on a one-to-one basis, revealing God's love to them through you.* (Plus Pages: Ideas for Activity Centers, *Preschool, Fall 1997,* © CPH *1997, page 3. All rights reserved.*)

The lesson plans that follow reflect this kind of bridgebuilding in steps 3 and 4.

KINDNESS FINDER

(Adapted from *Activity Center Time Booklet, Our Life in Christ,* Fall 1996, ©CPH 1996, page 8. All rights reserved.)

Concept: God helps people to love and forgive each other. God helps us to show kindness.

Prepare a "kindness finder" for each child. Cut a piece of red plastic wrap and use a rubber band or tape to attach it to the end of a cardboard tube.

Step 1	Activity	("Do It")

Give each child a "Kindness Finder" tube. Give them stickers and markers or crayons to decorate their tubes. Show how you use it, "When I see red, it reminds me that Jesus loves me. He forgives me, and He helps me to forgive others and be kind to them. Let's decorate our Kindness Finders." When the children have finished decorating, encourage them to look through their finders to find people being kind to each other.

Step 2	Process	("What?")

Ask individual children if they are seeing any kindness and where. Write down their responses, making a list of observations. (The children will not be able to read what you write. However, writing them indicates to the children that you have recognized and valued their responses.)

Step 3	Connection	("So What?")

Read the list of the children's observations. Say, "Here is what you saw through your Kindness Finders. Did anyone see anything else?" Write down what they tell you. Then ask, "This is a good list. What else might be some kind things you could do?" List those. Continue, "Our Bible story today tells us that God is kind. He sent Jesus to save us. Jesus is our best friend."

Step 4	Application	("Now What?")

Divide the class into two groups. Ask one group to go to the centers while the other group uses their Kindness Finders. Say,"Jesus helps us to be kind to one another. I wonder if we can find more kind things people are doing for each other." After a short time switch groups.

CHURCH FIELD TRIP

Bible Lesson: "I was glad when they said to me, 'Let us go into the house of the LORD!' " (Psalm 122:1 NKJV)

Field trips do not have to include travel. Several discovery journeys can take place right on church and school property. A favorite place is the church sanctuary. The following model shows a way to process the trip in an active learning cycle. This trip offers an overview of the entire church setting. Other trips could be more specific, focusing on Communion, Baptism, or music. Tour guides may include pastors, organists, or members of the altar guild.

Step 1	**Activity**	**("Do It")**

Plan to take the class to the church sanctuary. This may require extra helpers to assist watching the children en route. Tell the children they will be going to a wonderful place where they can look at things in a new way. Encourage them to look and listen. Remind them that there will be times when they will be able to touch things and times when they are not to touch things, and that you will let them know what things they will be allowed to touch. Explore the entire sanctuary as a group. Give everyone a chance to look closely at the following: the Baptismal font, the communion wear, the altar, the crosses, the banners, the stained glass, or whatever sacred appointments you find. Show where the lights are turned on and off and where the audio and visuals are controlled. Let the children look out from the lectern and pulpit. Let them see the musical instruments used for worship.

Step 2	**Process**	**("What?")**

Return to the classroom and ask the children to be seated. Explain that you now are going to listen to them talk about their trip. Tell them you want to record all their thoughts on a large poster page entitled: "What We Saw in Church." Tell them that they will need to take turns to share, and you will write what they say. This technique works with prereading children as a way to formalize their thoughts. You will notice that they can remember which words are theirs.

Step 3	Connection	("So What?")

Read the poster to the children and ask, "What did we like about the church? What was a surprise?" The children will not be able to speak as a group; yet they will recall more information that will help them to connect the experience to verbal skill building. Ask the children, "Are you glad when you go to church?" Listen to the responses. Do not comment on their statements. Open the Bible to the psalm and say, "Listen to what David wrote in the Bible. He was glad when he went to church."

Step 4	Application	("Now What?")

Say to the children, "I am so glad that we went to the church sanctuary today because I like to go to church. I am glad we got to see all the things that make our church special. Whom do you go to church with? What do you do in church? What can you tell your family about today's trip to church?"

DESCRIBING FEELINGS

Bible Lesson: One day as Jesus was standing beside the Lake of Gennesaret, with the people crowding around Him and listening to the Word of God, He saw at the water's edge two boats, left there by the fishermen, who were washing their nets. He got into one of the boats, the one belonging to Simon, and asked him to put out a little from the shore. *(Pause here.)* Then He sat down and taught the people from the boat.

When He had finished speaking, He said to Simon, "Put out into the deep water, and let down your nets for a catch."

Simon answered, "Master, we've worked hard all night and haven't caught anything. *(Pause here.)* But because You say so, I will let down the nets."

When they had done so, they caught such a large number of fish that their nets were beginning to break. *(Pause here.)* So they signaled their partners in the other boat to come and help them, and they came and filled both boats so full that they began to sink.

When Simon Peter saw this, he fell at Jesus' knees and said, "Go away from me, Lord; I am a sinful man!" *(Pause here.)* For he and all his companions were astonished at the catch of fish that they had taken, and so also were James and John, the sons of Zebedee, Simon's partners.

Then Jesus said to Simon, "Don't be afraid; from now on you will catch men." (Luke 5:1–10)

Step 1	**Activity**	**("Do It")**

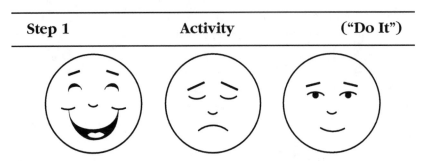

Make a set of three faces for each child. Cut out the faces and glue each of them to a craft stick. Give each child the three faces. Say, "Boys and girls, I am going to read you a story and you are going to help me by using your feeling faces. I will tell about a story about Peter and the disciples. You will show me how they are feeling in the story by holding up a face." Demonstrate for them by saying, "When Peter is sad, I would hold up this face. If he were happy, I would hold up this one."

Tell the story in your own words. Emphasizing the feelings. Use your expressions to help them. Pause at the points indicated and ask the children to show their faces.

Step 2	**Process**	**("What?")**

Say to the children, "When Peter was with Jesus, Peter had lots of different feelings. Feelings are important. Use your faces and show me what you feel like when the following happens:

> Your parent says, "Clean up your room."
> You fall and hurt yourself.
> Someone says, "I love you."
> Someone won't play with you.
> Someone gives you a hug.

Step 3	Connection	("So What?")

Show the happy face and say, "When Jesus sees you, He has this feeling. Show me the feeling you have when Jesus says to you, 'I love you.' " Go to each child one at a time and say, "I love you."

Step 4	Application	("Now What?")

Say to the children, "It's nice to know God gives us feelings and that He loves us. Did you know that in church the pastor ends the service with a special good-bye called the Benediction?

Sometimes the pastor says, "The Lord bless you and keep you. The Lord make His face shine on you."

"What do you think it looks like when God makes His face shine on us? Here is how I make my face shine." (Smile broadly at each child.) "Let's all let our faces shine on each other."

SHARE OUR FOOD

Bible Lesson: Mark 6:37 (before Jesus feeds more than 5,000 people with five loaves and two fish.) [Jesus] answered, "You give them something to eat."

They said to Him, "That would take eight months of a man's wages! Are we to go and spend that much on bread and give it to them to eat?"

Step 1	Activity	("Do It")

Show the children how to play the game of musical chairs. The children walk around chairs until the music stops. Then they all sit down. Do this three times to get the routine. Young children will enjoy this without removing any chairs. Then say, "What would happen if I took away half the chairs? *(Take away the chairs.)* Can you tell me what might happen?" Listen to their answers and repeat them back to them. "Let's do that once to see what happens." When half the children have taken their seats, group all the standing children together and say, "Look what happened. These children do not have seats. Could anyone who is seated move over a little and let someone sit down?" Some children will let their friends sit down, while others may still stand or refuse to move. Simply end the activity by saying, "Look. Because some shared, more people can sit down."

Step 2	**Process**	**("What?")**

Ask the following questions. "Did you like the game? Did you like to sit down? Did you like to share your chair?" Just listen to the responses. Do not evaluate or comment.

Step 3	**Connection**	**("So What?")**

If you have a normal snack time, wait until then to do this connecting experience. Choose a snack food that can be divided. Small apples or crackers work well. Have enough food for half the class. Place the pieces of food in the center of the table and say, "Before we say our prayer for snacks, I want to count the food and the children. You can help me count. Oh no! We don't have enough. There are more boys and girls than we have food.

"That happened to Jesus too. There were so many people, His friends didn't know what to do. They wanted to send the people home to eat, but Jesus asked, 'How much food do you have?' They brought only five loaves of bread and only two fish. Jesus took the food, broke it, and said a prayer. Then He told His friends, 'Give it to the people.' They did just that. Jesus make enough bread and fish for more than 5,000 people, and His friends shared it. There was even food left over.

"Now, what should we do?" The children will know they should divide the snack. Talk about that with them. Then move to the application.

Step 4	**Application**	**("Now What?")**

Continue the snack time. Say to the children, "Let's do what Jesus did." Say this prayer. "Thank You for our food. Help us to share what we have so that everyone has some."

After snack time ask if the children enjoyed the food. Then declare, "God did it again. He filled us with good things!"

AFRAID? ME?

Bible Lesson: Jesus walks on water (Matthew 14:22–33).

Step 1	Activity	("Do It")

Give each child some play dough or a piece of paper and a crayon. Ask them to make a shape of something that scares them or to draw it on paper.

Encourage any efforts by the children. Do not prompt them to achieve perfection in their sculptures or drawings. As they work, invite them to talk about what they are making/drawing.

Step 2	Process	("What?")

Invite each child to tell what scares him or her. Write their responses on the board. At first just listen and write. Then allow time for the children to express their fears. Assure them of God's unending love and care.

Step 3	Connection	("So What?")

Tell the story of Jesus and Peter walking on the water. (Try this additional active learning: Tape the shape of a boat hull on the floor of your classroom. Ask all the children to "sit in the boat." Choose someone to play Jesus and someone else to play Peter. Tell the children what actions you would like them to do to help you tell the story. For example, have them row their boats, scream with fear, and react in other ways to the story.)

Step 4	Application	("Now What?")

Now return to the responses you wrote on the board. Assure the children that just as Jesus protected Peter and the other disciples when they were afraid, so He also takes care of us. Ask the children to suggest ways to remember that Jesus is always with them—even when they're afraid.

Active Learning Designs: Primary

Every word of God is flawless; He is a shield to those who take refuge in Him. (Proverbs 30:5)

In early childhood children simply experience things. During the primary years they begin to reflect upon the experience, draw conclusions, and associate meaning. However, their thoughts still tend to be concrete in nature. They are likely to see things as black and white, right and wrong. Do not expect complex reasoning from these children.

The art of constructing and asking questions is a critical tool for active learning. Children in the primary years are just beginning to think in abstractions. With careful construction of questions we can assist them as they move toward more complex thought. Keep in mind that this thinking process takes time. Teachers need to allow enough wait time before rephrasing the question, offering a hint, or answering the question themselves and moving on to the next point.

EXERCISE

You will need a clock or a time keeper for this exercise.
Read these questions one at a time. Answer the question out loud *before 10 seconds pass.*

> How does the way you were taught affect the way you teach?
>
> Think about the Christian education at your church. What important things need changing?

Next, read these questions, one at a time. This time, answer out loud *in 30 seconds.*

> How will you teach differently as the result of new information you have received about teaching and learning?
>
> How do you feel when you ask a question in class and no one responds?

Reflect: After a question has been asked, respondents need time to think, choose, and then verbalize their answers. When you teach, are you waiting long enough for the students to answer? Watch the second hand of a clock and think how long you wait after a question. Is it five seconds? 10? 15?

Never ask two questions in a row without allowing the first to be answered.

Hint: Prepare your discussion questions before class. Write them on the board or on poster cards. Read and show the question to the students and then WAIT. WAIT for them to reflect. WAIT for them to discover. WAIT for them to think out the words. WAIT for the wonderful thoughts and ideas that will follow.

WHO IS THE LEADER?

Bible Lesson: "[John] sent them to the Lord to ask, "Are You the one who was to come, or should we expect someone else?"(Luke 7:19)

Step 1	**Activity**	**("Do It")**

Play a game called "Who Is the Leader?" Have the children seated in a circle on the floor. Join them and ask them to do everything you do. Do simple motions that they all will follow. For example, pat your head, clap your hands, pull your ears, wave your hand, or cross your legs. Once the children have practiced some motions, choose someone to be "it." Have "it" out of sight; then choose another child to be the leader. Invite "it" to stand in the center of the circle and see if she or he can discover who is the leader.

Play several rounds. Then say, "This time let's make it very difficult for the person who's "it." Let's all look at the leader as little as possible. Try to only glance at this person or look from the corner of your eye. When you see others change motions, follow their lead."

Step 2	**Process**	**("What?")**

Stop the game and say, "I would like to get your ideas about this game. I have a poster here titled 'Helpful Hints to Play Who's the Leader?' I would like to write, with a marker, all your hints."

Go around the room collecting and recording exactly what the children say.

Step 3	**Connection**	**("So What?")**

Encourage the children to look at all the hints on the list and ask, "Do you see any ways that we play follow the leader in real life?"

Accept responses. If they don't come up with the concept of following good leaders, ask, "I can imagine there are lots of leaders in your life. Some are good and some may be bad. What do you think?"

Step 4	Application	("Now What?")

Before reading the Bible passage to the children, give them the following background information. John wanted to follow the right leader, so he sent someone to talk to Jesus. Ask the children to brainstorm a list of things that make Jesus a great leader.

To conclude the activity, ask each child to come forward to the list you have made. Ask them individually to complete the following sentence, pointing to the word on your list that applies. "I am going to follow Jesus because He is ...."

ONE BODY

Bible Concept: Everyone is an important part of the body of Christ. You have a key role to play for the whole body to function. All gifts are significant. Don't hold back.

Scripture: 1 Corinthians 12:12–13. (We are one body in Christ.)

Step 1	Activity	("Do It")

Find a poster with a special message or picture of Christ. Cut it up into pieces like a puzzle. Cut one piece for each child. Make one piece very important (right in the center; a significant word or feature). Distribute the pieces of the puzzle to the children, but keep the "special" piece. Ask the children to put the puzzle together, one piece at a time. After everyone has taken a turn and as the frustration mounts, say things like, "Won't it be okay without the piece? Do you really think I can help? What good is my piece? It's only one out of many."

Step 2	Process	("What?")

Tell the children that you would like to ask what they were thinking and feeling about the puzzle. One at a time, ask each child for his or her thoughts. Write each thought on the board or on a large piece of paper. Tell students that it is all right if they would like to pass their turn. Conclude this section by supplying the missing piece.

Step 3	Connection	("So What?")

Ask, "What games or projects in your life require other people?"

Step 4	Application	("Now What?")

Say to the children, "The piece of the puzzle that I had was very important. Each one of you is important to Jesus. You may be small, but like the puzzle piece, we need you in this world to make things work according to God's plan."

Invite each child to come forward and take his or her puzzle piece. As you call individuals forward, complete this sentence, "You (child's name), are important to me because ...."

PUT-DOWNS TEAR DOWN

Bible Concept: When we put someone down, we are ripping away at that person's self-esteem. People can't do their best when they have low self-esteem. In Christ we are affirmed, and by His power we can affirm others.

Scripture: Philippians 2:3–7: Imitate Christ. John 15: Have the same love.

Step 1	Activity	("Do It")

Invite the children to draw a heart on a paper plate. Ask the class to think of things people can say to hurt our feelings. Go to each child and collect her or his thoughts. Write each child's idea in a word or two on the board or a large sheet of paper. Instruct the children to write their words on their plates in the part that is outside of the heart shape.

Now it gets exciting. You might want to move outside or into the gymnasium. Or, you may choose to stay in class and be creative with the space.

Show how the plate can be used as a flying disk (frisbee). In teams of two record how far (in steps) you can throw the plate. Give each child two tries.

GET ACTIVE

Get everyone's attention and say, "Now remember your distance and tear out one of the words that hurts. Throw that piece into the waste basket. Toss the plate and measure it again. Do this until all the words are gone and only the heart remains."

Step 2	**Process**	**("What?")**

Gather the children back into class at the chalkboard to record their thoughts.

Or, have them work in teams of four and use a marker to write a report on large sheet. "From This Game We Learned ...:" Give them a time limit of 5 minutes.

Step 3	**Connection**	**("So What?")**

Prepare a plate before class, like the children's, with a heart in the center. Write these words around the heart: *Friend, Branch, Fruit, Love, Joy,* and *Chosen.* Tear off each word and put a circle of masking tape on the back so it can be reconstructed during the following reading.

Read the following sentences as you put the appropriate piece back on the plate:

> *When people say, "You are no good." Remember what Jesus said to you, "I no longer call you servants, because a servant does not know his master's business. Instead, I have called you friends."* (John 15:15)
>
> *"If the world hates you, keep in mind that it hated Me first. I am the vine; you are the branches."* (15:18, 5a)
>
> *"If a man remains in Me and I in Him, he will bear much fruit; apart from Me you can do nothing."* (15:5b)
>
> *"If you obey My commands, you will remain in my love, just as I have obeyed My Father's commands and remain in His love."* (15:10)
>
> *"I have told you this so that My joy may be in you and that your joy may be complete."* (15:11)
>
> *"You did not choose Me, but I chose you and appointed you to go and bear fruit—fruit that will last. ... This is My command: Love each other."* (15:16a, 17)

Step 4	Application	("Now What?")

Lead the class in a guided imaginary. Ask them to close their eyes. It is critical that they close their eyes. Tell them to relax, and listen to your voice alone. Tell them to pretend and imagine. Read the following with 10 second pauses between them:

> Imagine you are walking outside on a warm spring day.
> As you walk, you see Jesus coming toward you.
> Somehow you just know it is Him, so you are not afraid.

> He comes up to you and, without talking, looks at you as if studying everything about you. He smiles a big smile and takes your hand.

> As you walk with Him, you notice another person coming into view. You know this person pretty well, but you do not get along with this person.

> You and Jesus walk up to the person. Jesus looks at that person and smiles the same way He smiled at you.

> Then Jesus joins hands with both of you. The three of you walk. It is warm and sunny, and you feel safe and secure.

> Now, Jesus stops and looks down at the two of you. Somehow you know you should hold hands with the other person too. Now you are standing holding hands in a circle.

> Jesus now puts His hands on your shoulders. Then somehow He disappears, leaving you holding the hand of your new friend.

Now open your eyes and hold the hand of the person next to you as we pray. "Thank You, Jesus, for making us friends in You."

DISCOVERY

(Adapted from *Plus Pages, Our Life in Christ,* Primary, Fall 1997, ©CPH 1997, page 4. All rights reserved.)

Concept: Creation. When we explore God's world, we discover how wonderful He is! "The heavens declare the glory of God; the skies proclaim the work of His hands" (Psalm 19:1).

Step 1	**Activity**	**("Do It")**

You will need cardboard boxes the size of shoe boxes or larger—one box for every two children in your class. Also, bring a variety of materials from nature such as rocks, leaves, shells, feathers, plants, seeds, pine cones, tree bark, and flowers.

Divide the class into pairs of children. Tell them, "You are going to play a guessing game with each other. One of you will look to see what is in the box. The other will have to guess what is in the box. The person who is guessing will have to ask questions about God's creation to discover what's in the box. The person who looks in the box may only answer questions with yes or no."

Switch sides and play a second time. Add new items to the boxes.

For the third round the pair needs to look for something very unique about each item. "Be ready to tell the class about it."

Step 2	**Process**	**("What?")**

Bring all the class together. Invite the pairs to tell about their items, one pair at a time. This will be like show and tell with the items they have just discovered.

Step 3	**Connection**	**("So What?")**

The Bible says that the creation declares the glory of God. That means that even silent things have a message from our heavenly Father. Ask, "Can you hear a message from the items you studied?" Write their responses on a large sheet titled "Silent Message."

Step 4:	**Application**	**("Now What?")**

Give each child a 3 × 5 index card with a hole punched in the center. Tell them that this can be a special viewer to see God's world. It helps you see just a small portion of something. Practice using the card to look at a small part of a larger item. Tell the class, "This week I would like you to look at three things with this viewer. Let me know what you discover. What did you learn about God's creation?"

PARABLE PLAY

Bible Lesson: "Laborers in the Vineyard" (Matthew 20:1–16), "The Sower" (Mark 4:2–9), or "Who Is My Neighbor?" (Luke 10:29–37).

Use this activity near the end of the primary grades, when the children can read and work independently. In this activity the children will lead the entire lesson. If you have 12 or more children, divide your class evenly into three groups. If you have 6–11 students, use two groups. If you have five or fewer children, keep them as one group and use a video camera to record the group's presentation. You will need to put up a blanket for a puppet stage.

Step 1	**Activity**	**("Do It")**

Announce to the class that they will be teaching the lesson today. They will work in teams to study parables and teach them to each other. Post the following rules and point them out to the class:

> You will each design a pantomime. You may use only the Bible and your hands.
> Everyone must be involved. One person will read the Bible parable, some can make sound effects, and everyone else will be characters in the pantomime.
> You will have 10 minutes to study the story and decide what each person will do.
> You will have 10 more minutes to prepare and rehearse.
> Then we will deliver our presentations.
> At the end of the presentation you will need to tell us what the parable means to your team.

Step 2	**Process**	**("What?")**

Bring the class back together to view the presentations. If you have one group, record the presentation on video tape. Then play it back on a monitor.

Watch all the presentations. Remind those in the audience to give their attention to those who are making their presentations.

Step 3	Connection	("So What?")

At the end of each presentation, the group will tell what the parable means to their team. Write group responses on the board to reinforce their learning.

Step 4	Application	("Now What?")

Ask the children to return to their teams and discuss the question, "How will you act differently this week because of what you learned?" Give them five minutes to develop an answer.

Remind the class that God gives us the desire and power to act according to His will.

Active Learning Designs: Intermediate

Day after day, in the temple courts and from house to house,
they never stopped teaching and proclaiming the good news that
Jesus is the Christ. (Acts 5:42)

IT'S ABOUT SELF-ESTEEM

What a joy Christian education can be. Unfortunately, some intermediate students no longer view school with joy, and their self-esteem is suffering. Parents and churches can close the self-esteem gap. Christian education can be a place where everyone succeeds, and Christian educators can set the standard for nurturing the whole child. However, a quality Christian education program does not include lowering of expectations in order to help all students feel good.

Self-esteem involves much more than feeling good. Christian self-esteem recognizes that God loves each individual—so much that He sent His only for us (1 John 4:10) and gave each of us special talents and gifts. Christian self-esteem is developed when love is shown and discipline takes place in the context of the students' baptismal relationship with God.

Christian teachers have the opportunity to bring—and keep—joy into the education process. Christian teachers who teach intermediate youth will find that they are ready for a challenge, for stimulation, for action, and that they long to be successful. The following lessons are designed in this spirit of joy.

CIRCLES OF INCLUSION

Bible Lesson: Luke 15:4–7. God cares about the lost. With His power, we care too.

Step 1	**Activity**	**("Do It")**

Say to the class, "I will call out a number. You must then join hands to form groups that have that exact number of people. Any people who are not in one of those circles must sit out. We will play until there are only two people standing."

You may need a whistle for this noisy activity.

Record the action on video, so you can play back the game. The person running the camera should be sure to get close-ups of the people who get left out.

Step 2	**Process**	**("What?")**

Play back the action. Simply ask the participants to write down words for the various feelings they observe.

If you don't have a camera, ask students to write the feelings they observed while playing the game.

Collect the sheets with the feeling words and record the words on the board or on a large sheet of paper.

Step 3	Connection	("So What?")

Say to the students, "The church is sometimes referred to as 'The Holy Huddle.' Would half of you please demonstrate what a football huddle looks like?" (Wait until they make the huddle.) "What does your church do to include new people in our 'huddle'? What do we do that shows rejection?"

Step 4	Application	("Now What?")

Continue, "Stay in your huddle as I read the Bible passage (Luke 15:4–7)." Now ask the same students to change the huddle. Each person in the huddle should turn and face out. Then ask each of them to go get one other person and form a new circle with everyone looking out.

Say "In the Bible passage you heard how much Jesus loves us. He searches for sinners, because He wants all of us included in His 'huddle' of those who are saved. His love gives us the power to reach out to include others in our huddles." Join hands and close with prayer.

"YOU ARE FORGIVEN" GAME

(Adapted from *Preteen Teachers Guide, Our Life in Christ,* September–November 1996, ©CPH 1996, pages 14–15. All rights reserved.)

Bible Concept: Jesus, who forgave Peter (John 21:15–19) and the Samaritan woman (John 4:1–26), also forgives us.

Before class begins prepare two brown lunch sacks, both double sacked (one sack inside another). Use a marker to write "Sin" on one sack and "Punishment" on the other. Leave the "sin" bag empty. In the "punishment" bag place white index cards with the word "Forgiven" on each one. Gather enough red and white index card so that each student in your class has one.

Step 1	**Activity**	**("Do It")**

You say to the students, "Today I will need your help to play the forgiveness game. I am going to give each you two index cards, a red one and a white one. On the red card write a sin that someone your age might commit. For example *(write these on the board or on a large sheet of paper)*:

> I told my parents a lie.
>
> I cheated on an important test at school. I got an A and I didn't deserve it.

Then think of a punishment that would be typical for that sin. Write it on the white cards. In other words, what could I do as your teacher? For example *(write these on the board or a large sheet of paper)*:

> Stand in the corner for five minutes.
>
> Write a one page essay on why you won't do it again.

Collect all the red cards and put them in the "sin" sack.

Collect all the white cards. *Hide them down the side of the doubled lunch sack titled "Punishment."* Before class practice hiding cards so you will be certain that they will be out of sight and that class members will not see where you are placing them.

Announce that it is time to administer punishments. Ask the students to come forward, one at a time. Take a card out of the "sin" bag and read it. Help students who cannot decipher the handwriting. Then say, "Take a card from the other sack and do what the punishment says."

Play this until everyone realizes that there are nothing but forgiveness cards in the sack.

Step 2	**Process**	**("What?")**

Listen only, as you collect comments from the students regarding the following open-ended questions.

> What did you think about the game when it first started?
> How did you feel when you realized that the "punishment" sack contained some "forgiveness" cards?

When did you first suspect that all the cards were "forgive-ness"?

| **Step 3** | **Connection** | **("So What?")** |

Ask, "Have you ever had the experience of doing something, getting caught, and not being punished for it? Would anyone be willing to tell about it?

How often do you think that happens in schools, families, and businesses?"

| **Step 4** | **Application** | **("Now What?")** |

Write on the chalkboard the following acronym:

G od's
R iches
A t
C hrist's
E xpense

Say, "By grace we are saved, through faith, it is a gift of God, not of works. No sin is so great that God will not forgive it. In a wonderful way His great love leads us to confess our sin and turn to Him for forgiveness. And, He always forgives us—His own dear children."

PRAYER TAKES SHAPE IN GROUPS

(Adapted from *Preteen Teachers Guide, Our Life in Christ,* September–November 1996, page 57, and *Plus Pages,* Page 10B, ©1996, CPH. All rights reserved.)

Bible Concept: "The prayer offered in faith will make the sick person well; the Lord will raise him up. If he has sinned, he will be forgiven. Therefore confess your sins to each other and pray for each other so that you may be healed. The prayer of a righteous man is powerful and effective" (James 5:15–16).

| **Step 1** | **Activity** | **("Do It")** |

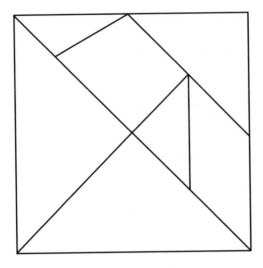

Photocopy this tangram, enlarged to about 8 inches square, onto tangram card stock paper. Cut out the tangram shapes. Have the students sit in groups of seven on the floor. Give a set of tangram pieces and a background page to each group. If your class is smaller than seven, divide the class into two even groups. Each student should have one tangram piece. You do not need to use every shape for this activity to succeed.

Give the following instructions. Do not hand out the materials until everyone understands the instructions.

"Each of you will get a shape. You will work with your group to create a design. Each group will get a background page. Create a design on that page.

"Each of you will take a turn, beginning with the person who is closest to me and going clockwise.

"Take some glue and glue your piece to the page and say, 'Please pray for me regarding ....' "

Add your shape to the others to make a unique design for prayer.

| **Step 2** | **Process** | **("What?")** |

Ask the teams to think of all the prayer requests and come up with a title that represents all the prayers. They should write that title on the art page. Then they should choose a representative who will show the design to the others.

| **Step 3** | **Connection** | **("So What?")** |

Ask the group representatives to come forward with the art work. Have them read the title and post the design with tacks or masking tape to a location you have selected.

| **Step 4** | **Application** | **("Now What?")** |

Say to the class, "God invites and encourages us to pray for each other and with each other. We do that in our church when we all pray together. We can also pray in small groups. And, always remember we can pray alone. God hears all our prayers for the sake of Jesus our Savior.

Let's pray right now." Lead the class in prayer or have class members take turns praying.

THE POWER OF THE SPIRIT AND WORD

Bible Concept: The Bible was written for us, even though we live many generations after Jesus. The Holy Spirit works faith in our hearts to believe in things we didn't see.

In John 17:20 Jesus prays to His Father, "My prayer is not for them [the disciples] alone. I pray also for those who will believe in Me through their message."

Step 1   **Activity**   **("Do It")**

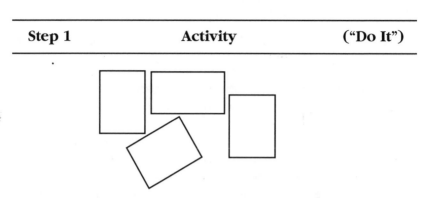

Give each class member four pieces of paper or index cards.Lay out four pieces of paper in a pattern on the table or floor. Ask your students if they believe they could lay out their pages in the same pattern. Have them do it.

Now lay out four pages in a new pattern, out of view of the students (in the hallway or closet). Ask them to do it again. But this time let them move to look at the model and come back to complete it. No pencils and papers are allowed.

Finally, have the students form teams of two. Have one person in each pair wear a name tag one with the letter A and the other the letter B. Change the unseen pattern by tearing the pages in two and scattering them on the floor. One child (A) will stay to lay out the cards while the other (B) goes to look and reports back information. Child B may not touch the pieces the cards. The cards must be laid out by child A.

Step 2   **Process**   **("What?")**

Record the students' thoughts on the board or on a large sheet of paper. Make two columns so that you can compare student A's comments with student B's comments. Tell the class that you are going to collect and record thoughts and feelings about each of the three ways to pattern cards. Encourage each person to share his or her ideas. Listen and record while managing the conversation.

| Step 3 | Connection | ("So What?") |

Lead the following discussion, "Look at the words we have used to describe the different ways you matched the cards. What is the main difference between the ways we did it?"

Take out a Bible and show it to them as you say, "Here is a book that has been copied and recopied for a long, long time. It has been translated into many different languages. None of us were there when the things in the Bible took place, so how can we know the Bible is true?

"Listen to this passage from the Bible." Read John 17:20. Jesus was praying for you and me. He knew that the written words and stories of Him and the disciples, who were eyewitnesses of Jesus, would cause believers to follow Him.

I know you believe in things you can't see. Can you think of some? We will write them down too."

| Step 4 | Application | ("Now What?") |

Say, "The Holy Spirit works faith in our hearts. We believe the Bible is true and that God's Word lasts forever. Above all, we 'believe in [Jesus] through their message,' and we are sure of life eternal."

Active Learning Designs:
Middle School to Adult

When I was a child, I talked like a child, I thought like a child, I reasoned like a child. When I became a man, I put childish ways behind me. Now we see but a poor reflection as in a mirror; then we shall see face to face. Now I know in part; then I shall know fully, even as I am fully known. And now these three remain: faith, hope and love. But the greatest of these is love. (1 Corinthians 13:11–13)

RELATIONSHIPS ARE IMPORTANT—VERY IMPORTANT

St. Paul says it well, "I put childish ways behind me." When youth reach early adolescence, they begin the process of putting away childhood. But by God's grace faith, hope, and love will remain in their lives. For teenagers, love is the central issue of their existence. This goes beyond a greater awareness of their sexuality; they have an ever deepening interest in relationships. The active learning process capitalizes on the teen's desire to interact with peers.

Adolescents are developing greater capacity for logic and abstract thinking. They begin to enjoy questions such as, "If God is all-powerful, can He make a rock so big He can't pick it up?" We tend to rejoice when we see them discover higher levels of reasoning. But adolescence has its more difficult moments as well, such as when they begin to question every rule and authority. What a great time for the church to be there and to celebrate, support, and nurture their growing faith.

Active learning designs for teenagers become more student-centered. The teacher remains passive and observant while guiding the youth to self-discovery and personal commitment. Some teachers have, successfully, given over the instruction to the class. This does not mean less work. In fact, more work is required to plan and coach and prompt the leaders. Many teachers, however, assure us that the rewards received from having students lead the classes make it well worth the effort.

MIDDLE SCHOOL TO ADULT

The following designs have a broad application. Because the lessons are student-centered, the class will take the discussion to the level of their readiness. Some of these designs have been used with adults, and some have been conducted with families. Do not expect the sixth graders and the adults to reach the same conclusions. Because of differing life experiences, differing age groups may interpret the same data in different ways. God enables all, however, to look from the perspectives of faith, hope, and love—especially love, as they grow in their faith.

FRIENDSHIP

Bible Lesson: Jonathan and David, based on selected readings from 1 and 2 Samuel.

Step 1	Activity	("Do It")

1. Ask participants to write down two or three qualities they look for in a friend.
2. Ask each person to share one quality from his or her list. Record it on newsprint or poster board.
3. Give each participant five self-adhesive signal dots or a marker. Tell them to mark their personal "top five."
4. Tabulate the marks and make a new list of the top 10 friendship characteristics.
5. Divide the class up into four groups. Assign a passage from the list below to each group. Tell them to read the passages, looking for the friendship qualities. Have them prepare to report back.

   1 Samuel 17:57–18:4
   1 Samuel 19:1–4
   1 Samuel 20:9–17
   1 Samuel 31:1–4 and 2 Samuel 1:10–12

Step 2	Process	("What?")

Have groups report back. Encourage them to give a brief account of what is happening in their section of the story. Ask them, "What qualities from our list did Jonathan and David demonstrate?" Have them draw a star next to those qualities on the "Top 10" chart.

Step 3	Connection	("So What?")

Ask, "How would you evaluate this class as a friendship group? What gets in the way? What are you going to do about it? What clue to friendship do you find in 1 John 4:19?"

| **Step 4** | **Application** | **("Now What?")** |

Say, "For our closing let's read 1 Corinthians 13. Some people call it the love chapter. Reflect upon the power for love that we receive through the love of Jesus!"

THINGS NOT SEEN

Bible Concept: What we have seen with eyes of faith we pass on to others so they too believe.
Scripture: John 20:29 (Jesus' words to Thomas)

| **Step 1** | **Activity** | **("Do It")** |

Construct an art sculpture out of a small number of children's construction toys. Place the "art" in another room or in a box secluded from the group. Divide the group into teams of two.

Give one person in each team the necessary materials to make the replica. A partner will be able to look at the "art" as often as he or she wishes, but may not make the replica. The partner just *tells* the other person how to do it.

Increase the tension by offering prizes to the first team to complete it perfectly. Set your watch to record how long it takes. However, do not tell them you have timed it.

| **Step 2** | **Process** | **("What?")** |

Say to the group, "Please talk about your experience in your pairs before we discuss it as a large group. Answer the following questions." (Write them on the board.)

What frustrated you the most about the task?

How did the frustrations of the one making the "art" differ from those of the partner?

If you did this again, how would you improve your time?

Put a new art sculpture in the room or box and have them try to improve their time.

Step 3	Connection	("So What?")

Read or tell in your own words John 20:19–29. Ask, "How does this connect to our activity? How does it match some of the frustrations you felt? What connections can you make between this activity and the real-life activity of telling others about Jesus?"

Step 4	Application	("Now What?")

Say to the group, "I would like you to write five ways you, personally, could make Jesus 'more real' to your friends. After you have worked alone for three minutes, I will collect your thoughts on newsprint. Then we will work as a group to develop a list of the 'Top 10 Ways to Help Others See Jesus.' Next week I will bring a printed copy and I will also submit it for our church newsletter."

NEW LIFE IN A GRAVEYARD (FIELD TRIP)

Bible Concept: New life (John 11:1–44, Jesus raises Lazarus from the dead)

Step 1	Activity	("Do It")

Take your group to a cemetery. Be sure to first check with the caretaker. Gather the group in the middle of the graveyard. Say, "This is a sacred place for people who have their loved ones buried here. Please use discretion and respect for this space."

"We will gather thoughts and feelings. Then we will let God's Word speak to us."

Give each participant some butcher paper, charcoal, and crayons. Tell them, "Find a headstone that is particularly interesting to you. Place the butcher paper over the stone. Lay the charcoal or crayon flat on the paper. With long even strokes rub across the paper until you have a relief print of the headstone. If the relief shows a Bible passage, look it up. Be prepared to share your rubbing with the others.

| **Step 2** | **Process** | **("What?")** |

Say, "We are first going to look at the impressions you made on the paper. Then we will ask you what impressions it makes on you. Tell me, what are your thoughts and feeling right now?"

| **Step 3** | **Connection** | **("So What?")** |

After all have had an opportunity to share their thoughts and feelings, tell them, "Listen as I read the account of Jesus raising Lazarus from the dead. Imagine it happened here. Choose a grave to stare at while you picture it happening. Be aware of the feelings that are expressed by the people in the story. Be reminded that there is the body of someone who was loved and cared for lying here in this place." Review the incidents in John 11 that lead up to your reading. Then read the last portion (perhaps verses 17–44 or 32–44) from the Bible.

| **Step 4** | **Application** | **("Now What?")** |

Ask, "What is your favorite Easter hymn? What would you like to have written on your headstone?"

PLEASE, NO UNDERCOVER CHRISTIANS!

Bible Concept: There is only one Lord, one faith, one Baptism. We do not want to keep this a secret.

> *You are the light of the world. A city on a hill cannot be hidden. Neither do people light a lamp and put it under a bowl. Instead they put it on its stand, and it gives light to everyone in the house. In the same way, let your light shine before men, that they may see your good deeds and praise your Father in heaven.* (Matthew 5:14–16)

| **Step 1** | **Activity** | **("Do It")** |

Play one of those games where a few people know how to do the game or solve the mystery.

For example, play "Going on a Picnic." The leader says, "I'm going on a picnic, and I'm taking a *kite* and a *beach ball*. Who else would like to go? What will you bring?" The leader gives a secret code to a few others, and they reinforce the mystery.

In this case the leader used the initials from his name to choose the items for the picnic: *kite* for Kurt, and *beach ball* for Bickel. When someone gets it right and says the sentence correctly, the leader says, "You may go! Who else wants to go?"

Play the game long enough to build frustration for those who do not know what is going on. You might even say things like, "This is so easy. Once you know it, you'll be so embarrassed. ... I have played this with kindergarten children, and they have figured it out. ... You probably aren't listening very closely."

After a while, give some clues, such as "Listen very carefully to who is saying what. ... Here is a great clue: some people won't get it initially."

End the game and tell everyone what the secret is.

| **Step 2** | **Process** | **("What?")** |

Say to the participants, "I wanted to play that game to make a point, but before you guess the point, think about your feelings at the beginning, middle, and end of the game. Write your answers to the following questions."

> How did you feel about the leader?
>
> How did you feel about those who knew the secret?
>
> What did you feel about yourself?
>
> How did you feel about the game?

| **Step 3** | **Connection** | **("So What?")** |

Say, "Some people act as though their faith is a secret. Get in groups of four or five and prepare a report on newsprint with markers. You have five minutes. Develop an answer to this question: *Imagine you are outside the family of faith. How would that be like the game? How is it different?*"

| **Step 4** | **Application** | **("Now What?")** |

As participants talk about sharing their faith, ask, "Why do you want others to know what you believe?" Encourage responses that point out the eternal consequences for those without faith, and the love we have for others that leads us to want them to be saved.

End with a candlelighting ceremony. Place as many candles on an altar as you have participants. Remind students to exercise caution with the open flames. Place a large candle in the center of the group. Light the large candle and say, "Jesus is the light of the world. Let's each take a turn lighting our candles and saying, 'I will let my light shine by ...' " As leader, you take the first turn.

Design Your Own Active Learning

The Spirit helps us in our weakness. We do not know what we ought to pray for, but the Spirit Himself intercedes for us with groans that words cannot express. (Romans 8:26)

You need to utilize your right brain to design active learning. This means you will need to see, feel, and hear the lesson. You will need to think without words. To plan inductive experiences, you will need to think and plan backwards.

THE BACKWARD DESIGNING PROCESS

When *designing* active learning, you reverse the steps of the teaching process. During the active learning cycle you end with the Bible passage. When *planning* the lesson, you start there. After you study the Bible passage, you think of applications. Then think how will this connect, and then you brainstorm possibilities. Finally, you design the activity.

Bible Lesson or Concept: Begin the designing process by studying the Bible passage. Answer the following questions:

> Who wrote this?
>
> To whom was it addressed?
>
> What was the key message?
>
> What does the passage say about the sinful human condition and about God's grace?
>
> How does this passage connect to the message of Jesus as Savior?
>
> What is the central truth of this passage?

Step 1	**Plan the Application**	**("Now What?")**

> What *one* central truth do I want to emphasize, and how will I phrase it so participants will understand it?
>
> How will participants be different because of this lesson? How will they think differently? How will they feel differently? How will they act differently?
>
> With what words of encouragement can I dismiss them?

Step 2	**Plan the Connection**	**("So What?")**

Think about your participants. How does the lesson theme connect to their world, to their family and relationships?

> What reminders of their sinful condition do they need to hear?
>
> How can they best hear the words of the Gospel?

What questions could I ask them to stimulate their thinking about this passage?

What question could be answered differently by each student?

How will I honor their unique thoughts?

Step 3	Plan the Process	("What?")

This step is your creative process. Explore ways to actively convey the central truth you would like to teach. Here are some right brain exercises that may help in your process.

Keep your central theme in focus while you pray about it. Use a sandwich prayer. (Read the Bible passage; pray; read the passage again.)

Keep your central theme in focus and begin sketching the words in symbols and pictures.

Close your eyes. Imagine the faces of your class members as they hear and deeply understand the message.

What do *you* feel when you hear this message? What occurrences in your life caused similar feelings?

What might happen in your students' lives to create similar feelings?

If there were no limitations of space or money, what could you do? Could you go on a deep sea fishing trip ... dress in real camel hair ... have a complete sound and video stage ... do the challenges of a three ring circus?

Step 4	Plan the Activity	("Do It")

Design your own special activity or choose an activity from this chapter, from your curriculum, or from other resources. The activity should meet the following criteria:

Relates to one theme or central truth.

Involves all class members.

Involves physical motion.

Stimulates feelings.

PROBLEMS AND CHALLENGES

Jesus spoke all these things to the crowds in parables; He did not say anything to them without using a parable. So was fulfilled what was spoken through the prophet: "I will open My mouth in parables; I will utter things hidden since the creation of the world." (Matthew 13:34–35)

In many circles active learning has received a bad reputation over the years. Much of it is justly deserved. Some teachers planned action for the sake of activity.

Active learning is a specialized skill. The activity is not technically difficult. However, processing the activity with discussion and keeping the focus on the students requires practice and intuitive knowledge. Teachers should not simply prepare the activity without carefully planning the follow-up. Successful and effective lessons require a carefully planned and well-processed follow-up.

WITHOUT THE PROCESSING, ACTIVE "LEARNING" IS EMPTY ACTIVITY

One excellent example of pointless activity comes from the author's first year of teaching a confirmation class.

I taught a unit on The Ten Commandments to a group of 15 or so seventh graders. I had covered the lessons from the textbook and included memorization of the commandments with Luther's explanations. I promised the class that when we completed the unit, we would have an outdoor recreation time.

It was a wonderful fall day in St. Joseph, Missouri. I took the class to the parking lot for a game of kick ball. I had explained to the youth that this game would follow some simple rules:

—Everyone must participate.

—Instead of three outs, everyone would kick each inning.

—You get one pitch. If you miss or kick it foul, you are out.

—I will be the pitcher for both teams.

—When you come to the plate, I will ask you to recite a commandment. If you say it correctly, I will pitch you the ball. If you do not know it, you are out. (Are we having fun yet?)

—We will play until the bell rings.

James Kline came to the plate. "James," I said, "what is the Second Commandment?"

James was a bright student who responded sharply, "Thou shalt not take the name of the Lord, thy God, in vain."

I asked, "What does this mean?"

To which James replied in machine-gun rhythm, "We should fear and love God that we may not curse, swear, use witchcraft, lie, or deceive by His name, but call upon it in every trouble, pray, praise, and give thanks."

"Perfect," I said as I rolled the soccer ball his way.

James kicked it long into foul territory.

"You're out," I shouted.

In that split second, as clear as a bell, as if all the other playground noise was somehow muted, I heard James take God's name in vain.

I paused in disbelief. Then I shouted with pious anger, as only rookie teachers can, "You are out! Your team is out! Everyone is out! Back to the classroom! I will want to talk to you there!"

Later I wondered, how could James memorize it perfectly and miss the point? And what was the point of playing kick ball? It would have been a better celebration without the memory work, for sure. Jim Kline, wherever you are, I forgive you. I pray you have forgiven me too.

This story illustrates a major challenge related to teaching the faith: knowledge without application. While only God's power could have led James not to take God's name in vain, little in the passive or active learning experiences had served to prepare him for that moment.

Intentional active learning provides the connections between words, meanings, and actions. Reading the Bible with active learning becomes a tool for the Holy Spirit to build faith and empower students for God-pleasing lives.

50 MORE ACTIVE IDEAS

These additional ideas can help teachers design their own lesson plans.

To the new teacher: The following activities are not be used as a stand-alone component of your class, somehow shoehorned into the lesson. Look back to the beginning of this chapter and see how to design your lesson around them.

To the veteran, student-centered teacher: You may be a highly successful teacher on a scavenger hunt, looking for good ideas. Great! Active teachers continue to refine, reshape, pick and choose, until they have a style and method that best suits them. Successful teachers are eclectic. May you find something helpful for your toolbox.

1. **Spelling Bee.** Explore the vastness of God's mercy. Have a spelling bee. Give the same nice prize to the first one to sit down as to the last one standing.

2. **Play Dough.** Work the dough with your hands while you hear the Bible story. Then make a play dough model of your favorite part.

3. **Junk Sculpture.** Have the students make a sculpture to represent the discarded relationships in their lives. This junk reminds me of … and I put it here on the pile, next to this, because …

4. **Field Trip to a Junk Yard or Landfill.** A sensory awareness trip class members won't forget. Compare the trash heap to Golgotha.

5. **Scarf Drama.** Use colorful, silky, flowing scarves to tell a story from the Bible, such as the creation, the flood, or the Red Sea crossing.

6. **Banners.** Express thoughts, moods, and feelings in banners. Groups can work together. Don't limit yourself to cloth. Paper, cellophane, waxed paper, and foil all make great textured banners.

7. **Overhead Projector.** This is a great little tool. Give students clear sheets on which to draw background scenes. Then cut out paper characters to lay on the scene, like on a flannel graph. Imagine reenacting the flood .. with a blue sheet rising up … and that ark floating.

8. **Construction Toys.** These have great possibilities for giving shape to unexplained actions of God.

9. **Rhythmic Movement.** This can be effective at all levels, not only for preschools.

10. **Hidden Talent.** Everyone writes on an index card—or whispers into the teacher's ear, who writes—a talent they have that others may not know about. The teacher mixes up the cards and reads them as everyone guesses whose it is.

11. **Song Writing.** Write a song to a familiar tune. A song about friendships could be sung to the "Flintstones" theme music.

12. **Observation Deck.** Place assorted items (covered) on a table. Uncover briefly to let the students look at them. Then cover again. See who remembers what or how many each person can remember alone. How many were remembered by someone when working alone? How many more can the class remember when the group works together?

13. **Painting.** Create a large group mural. Add to it with every new learning and story. Put large sheets of paper on the walls, everywhere. Spread newspaper on the floor for easy clean up. Use lots of colors and lots of ways to apply it.

14. **Famous Names.** Write the names of well-known biblical characters on paper that you can tape to the backs of students. Have them try to guess who they are by asking questions that can be answered only with yes or no.

15. **Slide and Video Presentations.** This project can last for several weeks with great results. Choose a popular Christian hymn. Give it modern pictures and symbols. Or, take a popular secular song and give it Christian symbols and interpretation.

16. **Time Line.** Do a time line of your life. Show the ups and downs. Do a time line of a biblical person and show his/her ups and downs.

17. **Puppets.** Children make them for telling stories and for self-expression.

18. **Put It on a Roll.** The whole class draws sequential pictures of an experience they had together. The teacher tapes it together and pulls it through a specially made viewing box. This often works better than television.

19. **Strength Bombardment.** Each student gets into the center of the class circle while everyone says nothing but positives about them. The teacher can lead the way to a warm and accepting environment.

20. **Rhythm Instruments.** Consider juice harps, kazoos, wash tub bass, finger cymbals, bongos, blocks, and tambourines. Put them in groups. Conduct them until a junior conductor is ready to take the baton.

21. **Breaking Bias.** Choose a topic (anything) that separates people. Then divide the group into two groups. Have them work in separate rooms. Have the first group develop a list of what they think are the problems that separate the groups. Have the second group develop a list of what they think the first group will see as the problems. Sin is still in the world, and sin divides. Bring the groups together and attempt to develop insights that will help class members deal with bias in their lives.

22. **Class Evaluation.** Give the students a chance to conduct an evaluation of your teaching. Be ready to listen, and slow to speak. After the evaluation involve the students in planning class activities—always working with appropriate Bible stories and concepts.

23. **Value Auction.** Give play money to class members. Have them to use it to purchase the goodies you have listed: *Knowledge, freedom, faith, peace, love,* and others you select. Younger children understand how to do this too.

24. **Competitive Building.** Two teams compete for highest, or longest, or strongest structure. Some cooperation may happen if you state the goal in a way that leaves it open for the groups to combine resources.

25. **Brain Teasers.** These can become active learning when you connect group work or some simulation with them. Worksheets alone are low in faith-building nutrition and high in precious time consumption.

26. **Learning Centers of All Kinds.** For example, have a truck load of sand dumped on a barricaded portion of the church parking lot. Go to Mt. Sinai, Jericho, or the Red Sea. A high school class could construct the walled city of Jerusalem for Holy Week. Play with the sand, and then have someone come and take it away. (That is another lesson.)

27. **Time Capsule.** Use for values clarification. This could be perfect for the year 2000.

28. **Masks.** Think about your many moods. Draw a mask and wear it during a class confessional service. Remove it at the absolution.

29. **Magazines.** Cutting out pictures is still an outstanding self-exploration technique. Help your students to just browse and feel, rather than hunt and seek.

30. **Wallets and Purses.** Ask class members to take one thing from their wallet or purse that they would not want to give away.

31. **Favorite Places.** Have students draw their favorite room in their house. Or, imagine going to their favorite place out of doors. Or, select their favorite channel on television or radio.

32. **Game Show.** The format of TV game shows lends itself to active learning. The students already know the rules. You can change the content to match the issue.

33. **Cooking.** The process of gathering, preparing, cooking, and eating offers many points of sensory interaction. Distribute all the items of a complex recipe and have the group prepare and cook it properly. **Be careful to avoid situations where students could burn or injure themselves in the process.** After they have eaten the food, compare the actual recipe and see how close they were.

34. **Interviews.** You can gather opinions on anything. This stimulates the participants' views and values as they conduct the interview. The topics don't have to be controversial to be informative.

35. **Class Newsletter.** Recruit several students or their parents to bring in their computers. Create a newsletter. Most software allows you to import files, so many contributors can participate.

36. **Toys.** You can never be too old for toys. Bring in your favorites. After everyone gets a chance to play, have class members brainstorm ways the toy reminds them of Jesus and the Christian faith. Give your top ideas to the pastor for the next children's talk.

37. **Trust Walk and Physical Challenge.** Perhaps you have already conducted a trust walk. One student is blindfolded and the other leads that student. Also consider simple team and group challenges. For example, have two students sit on the floor back to back. Tell them to link their arms together at the elbows. Then tell them to stand up without letting go.

38. **Walk a Mile in My Chair.** Bring wheelchairs to church and have your class navigate the obstacle course of your church property. Include a trip to the bathroom.

39. **Servant Events**. Servant events are direct, purposeful activities that provide lessons in discipleship. For example, prepare, serve, and clean up the coffee for the fellowship hour.

40. **Boxes.** Ask an appliance distributer to save big boxes for you, the more the better. Build tunnels, mazes, walled cities, and personal spaces in your classroom. One class kept the foldaway boxes for weeks while they decorated them inside and out. Each child would go into the private box and add to the reflection collection. In addition to other benefits, this can be a reminder that baby Jesus was laid in a feed box, the ark was a floating zoo box, and the ark of the covenant was a golden treasure box.

41. **Stars.** You don't have to go to the planetarium to study stars. Involve your group in a study of the nighttime sky. The Bible has wonderful references to stars. So much can be learned by exploring space from our earth-bound observatory. The Epiphany season is a good time for this experience.

42. **Animals.** For city children an up-close encounter with an animal has a lasting impression. For Bible references sheep and donkeys should be at the top of the list. I am a lamb of the Lamb.

43. **Lights.** How many different lights are there? What do they do? Make a list. Read John 1. How do the different lights point to Jesus.

44. **Water.** Begin at the beginning. Water is a central theme in the Bible. Send groups to explore at the level of their capability. The more they learn about water the more they will marvel at the God of Creation, the Flood, the Red Sea, the Water in the Wilderness, Baptism and the one who says, "I am Living Water."

45. **Finger Paint.** This needs to be lifted up for teachers who think it's for early childhood only. The next time you make pudding, put some on a serving tray and have fun. Clean up is easy and tasty. Finger paint while you are praying.

46. **Shopping.** Get some adult assistants. Bring your shopping list to class. Ask students to help. Divide into teams. Give them spending limits. Shop.

47. **Guided Imagery.** Say, "Close your eyes, relax, listen only to my voice." This is not hypnotism; it is meditation. When guided by the teacher, it can produce wonderful data for reflection and introspection. Keep it light. Keep it positive.

48. **Shadow Drama.** Take a king-sized bed sheet and an overhead projector. Read the story and act it out. When students are behind the sheet and in front of the light, you will find a new dimension in fun. Being David and Goliath is no problem. David stands near the sheet and Goliath near the light.

Swords and slings can easily be made from several readily-available materials.

49. **Kings, Queens, and Servants.** Choose some class members to be kings and queens. When they arrive, put crowns on their heads or chains round their necks. Explain that in everything you do that day, the servants will serve the kings and queens.

50. **Dreams.** Ask students to draw their dreams. Tell the story of Joseph.

CONDITIONS FOR CREDIT

1. No fewer than six 60-minute class sessions shall be held.
2. Attendance at 75% of the class sessions shall be required.
3. At least one hour of preparation shall be requested of all students in advance of each of the class sessions.
4. The textbooks and instructor's guides recommended by the Department of Child Ministry, 1333 S. Kirkwood Road, St. Louis, MO 63122-7295, shall be used.
5. An instructor other than the pastor ought to be approved by the local pastor in order to obtain credit for students. This approval shall be indicated by the pastor's signature on the application blank for credit.
6. The application for credit should be sent to the Department of Child Ministry immediately after the completion of the course.

APPLICATION FOR CREDIT

To be sent to   Department of Child Ministry
1333 S. Kirkwood Road, St. Louis, MO 63122-7295

Name of congregation: _____

Address of Congregation: _____
(Street and number or R. F. D.)

_____
(City)   (State)   (Zip)

Name of course for which credit is desired: _____

Dates on which lessons were conducted:_____

_____

Length of class sessions in minutes: _____

Number registered in class: _____

The persons on the following list have met all the requirements of attendance and preparation for class work, and are recommended to receive credit.

(Signed) _____ Instructor

(Signed) _____ Pastor

Date: _____

If the instructor of the course is not the pastor of the congregation, there should be two signatures: The instructor's and the pastor's.

(Please type or print)   _____
                         Last Name   First Name

_____

	Last Name	First Name
1.	_____	_____
2.	_____	_____
3.	_____	_____
4.	_____	_____
5.	_____	_____
6.	_____	_____
7.	_____	_____
8.	_____	_____
9.	_____	_____